*Happy Cooking!*

# Nantucket's Bounty

**Katie Barney Moose**

**Conduit Press**
**Annapolis, MD**

I am indebted to my husband, George, daughter, Lucinda and mother for encouraging me to write a Nantucket cookbook and share a number of family recipes. In 1982 my sister, Lili Perrin and cousin Betsy Hayes gathered many family recipes into two booklets that were given out to family members. On George's part, the Lay-Hall Family Cookbook, "Now Let us Praise Fried Pies" was edited by his cousin, Leila Ryland Swain and published by the Hall Printing Company in Marietta, Georgia. Thank you all for helping our book finally get published.

This book is dedicated to my mother and father without whom I would not be here, or have spent so much time on the island.

Conduit Press also wishes to thank Lucinda Holmes and Katherine K. Barney for proofreading "Nantucket's Bounty".

Front cover design: Jean Harper Baer

Copyright ©2000   Conduit Press

Published by Conduit Press, 111 Conduit Street, Annapolis, Maryland 21401.

Library of Congress Cataloging-in-Publication Data

Printed and Bound by Victor Graphics, Inc., Baltimore, Maryland, USA

ISBN: 0-9666610-5-2

# Table of Contents

Introduction                                             2

Historical Facts about Nantucket and its Food            4

Historic Inns and Taverns                               11

Nantucket Baskets                                       17

Appetizers                                              18

Special Drinks                                          40

Soups                                                   49

Seafood                                                 61

Fowl                                                    84

Meats                                                   94

Vegetables                                             107

Salads                                                 128

Pastas and Rice                                        147

Breads, Biscuits, and Coffee Cakes                     162

Egg and Brunch Dishes                                  171

Sandwiches                                             181

Chutneys, Jams, Sauces, Oils and Butters               191

Desserts                                               205

Index                                                  239

About the Author and Photographer                      251

# Pictures

| | |
|---|---|
| Nantucket Sunrise | 1 |
| The author, age 3 | 2 |
| Barnacle Kitchen | 4 |
| Nantucket Sunset | 18 |
| Nantucket Vineyards | 40 |
| Brant Point | 49 |
| Lobster Boat – Straight Wharf | 61 |
| Hadwen House | 84 |
| Ham and Biscuits | 94 |
| Vegetables | 107 |
| Salad Bowl and Nantucket Basket | 128 |
| Nantucket Harbor | 147 |
| Old Mill | 162 |
| Old North Wharf | 171 |
| Dionis | 181 |
| The Barnacle | 191 |
| Strawberry and Blueberry Trifle | 205 |

*"Tell me what you eat,*
*and I will tell you what you are."*
**Anthelme Brillat-Savarin (1755-1826)**

**Nantucket Sunrise**

1

# Introduction

Nantucket has been in my blood since I was introduced to the island for my first Thanksgiving, staying with my grandmother Barney at her house on Orange Street. Since that time I have reappeared every summer except for two, and spent the winter of 1994-95 there.

**The author on her third birthday at Orange Street**

Our family, on both sides, dates back to the original settlers. My parents met on Nantucket on August 12, 1944 and my father proposed on August 13th. They were married on September 25 and spent their honeymoon on Nantucket at the Barnacle, our family home on Swain's Wharf. My mother and father, it turned out, were sixth cousins, descendants of the Starbucks. Now as I walk or drive around Nantucket I realize a large number of houses were built by my family. Sadly only two remain with us now. But my family were Nantucketers through and through, with my grandfather Barney being the last born on the island in 1861. I just wish all four of my grandparents were around to retell the stories of Nantucket through the last one hundred plus years.

Over the years I stayed with one set of grandparents or the other. My grandmother Barney loved to take us for long walks after dinner, often to the Old Mill or Old Gaol, where she would regale us with the story of her being locked up by the last gaol keeper. She then would scurry us back home to blueberries and ice cream or Indian pudding for dessert, and then to bed with a Nantucket story book, usually one of Tony Sarg's delightfully illustrated tales.

Sunday dinners were often spent at "Oversea", my grandparent Kennedy's on The Cliff. We had to be dressed and arrive for dinner promptly at 1 o'clock, no matter where we were - beach, tennis court, or just having come from church. Other times we might be taken by grandparents or Cousin Marge Swain to "The Skipper" or "The White Elephant". "The Skipper" was always our favorite as we could sit outside, watch the boats coming and going, and feed the seagulls. Many an eye was dampened when that relic was torn down.

In the evening there would be beach parties. I remember some of the parties at Dionis and the watermelon cut out and filled, I think with a vodka punch? Sitting around a bonfire we'd sing "Michael Row Your Boat Ashore", "The Sloop John B", and other nautical or popular tunes. These were carefree days. Life seemed so much more simple then. No rush to get anywhere. In fact 'Sconset was at the other end of island, and since few families had more than one car, transportation out there was at times difficult or not possible.

Nantucket has changed a great deal since that time. However, we all soon return to our beloved island. Just remember to throw 2 pennies overboard, so you can return again.

# Historical Facts on Nantucket and its Food

The Barnacle kitchen when Uncle Alanson Barney owned the house
on Swain's Wharf

*"With the landless gull, that at sunset folds her wings and is rocked to sleep between billows; so at nightfall the Nantucketer, out of sight of land, furls his sails, and lays him to his rest, while under his pillow rush herds of walruses and whales."*
Herman Melville, "Moby Dick" (1819-91)

The history of Nantucket is intertwined with that of New England, where many of the traditional American dishes use ingredients such as wild turkeys, corn, potatoes, beans, squash, clams, scallops, cranberries and pumpkins, all of which were unfamiliar to the American colonists. The Indian names still proliferate on the island, each with its particular meaning. Those pertaining to food include Tuckernuck meaning "Loaf of Bread".

Nantucket Island is located 30 miles out to sea from Cape Cod. Known as the "Little Gray Lady", the first English settlers arrived at Madaket in 1659. Bartholomew Gosnold was the first Englishman to land on the island in 1602 at Sankaty Head. In 1659 Thomas Mayhew, Sr. of Martha's Vineyard sold Nantucket to the original ten purchasers, who in turn had to purchase the island from Native Americans.

Some of the early settlers on Nantucket were Quakers, who lived a life of simplicity, or others seeking religious freedom in the colonies. The earliest European settlers on the island, beginning with Thomas Mayhew, raised sheep. However, the English Woolens Act of 1699 forced the settlers to pursue other livelihoods. The families included the Coffins, Folgers, Bunkers, and Gardners. Peter Foulger (Folger), grandfather of Benjamin Franklin was one of the early Christian "missionaries". Among these families were prosperous owners from the Mainland, such as Thomas Macy. The Quaker movement was led by Mary (Coffin) and Nathaniel Starbuck, and their son Nathaniel Starbuck. The author's parents are both Starbuck descendants.

Fishing was important for survival, not only for the Native Americans, but also to the early settlers. They had to learn to salt and dry their fish, and live off the meager harvest of whatever they were able to raise on the island. It was no wonder then, that Nantucket, early on got involved in whaling. The Indians had caught right whales just offshore in canoes. Now the settlers, six men to a boat, one a harpooner, began to take on this dauntless task. In 1660-70s Nantucket began its whaling industry.

Ichabod Paddock was brought over from Cape Cod and divided the island into four whaling stations, with three more added c1700.

The town of Nantucket was named Sherburne from 1673 to 1795. In 1671 the island was incorporated as Nantucket and became part of New York Province. In 1673 Royal Governor Francis Lovelance renamed it Sherborn (Sherburne). The island became part of the Massachusetts colony in 1692, and received its present name in 1795.

The Oldest House was built on Sunset Hill in 1686 as a wedding present for Jethro and Mary Gardner Coffin. "Sconset and Sesachacha were fishing villages and were settled long before much of the rest of the island. 'Sconset was founded c1676. Below the Bluff in "Sconset is Codfish Park, once home to fishermen, later an artist's colony, and now sadly being eaten away by the sea Off here were good fishing grounds for cod, flounder, blackfish, sea bass, perch and other fish. Whale houses were built facing the Atlantic Ocean.

The first grist mill was built in 1666 at Lily Pond and in 1673 a tidal mill. In 1675 the Nantucket Court specified no corn could be taken off island, except to New York of which Nantucket was then a part. Plots then were planned by the town to grow wheat, rye, turnips, barley and vegetables. The Old Mill was built in 1746 by Nathan Wilbur. In 1802 a mill was built on New Lane. The millstone is now the foundation for the Civil War Monument at the top of Main Street By 1897 there had been 5 windmills on the island. Corn didn't grow in abundance. Islanders were lucky to get 50 bushels an acre, whereas on the mainland farms yielded 80 to 100 bushels.

Nantucket had a number of laws pertaining to the consumption of food and liquor. By law no alcohol, or even cider was to be sold to the Indians. As early as 1694 a white man was convicted of selling rum to the Indians. John Swain (1633-1715) of Polpis had among his inventory a house, barn, kitchen, milk room, and malt house, plus a license to operate a filling mill in Polpis. In his will Mr. Swain left his still to his wife. Thomas Brock (1698?-1750), a settler from Scotland, also built a distill house on his property in Wesco and owned a store. In 1761 a law prohibited minors from being entertained at unreasonable hours. In 1792 a Quaker was censured for cooking supper in his house on the Sabbath. An alcohol prohibition law was adopted in 1852 in Massachusetts.

Tea was introduced to the islanders in the late 17th c, but did not become popular until about 1750. Chinese and English porcelains were brought to the island, but the earliest teapots were made of pewter or silver. The Chinese trade was to become very important when seal skins were traded for luxury items in Canton, beginning in the late 1700s and ending in the 1830s. William Rotch's ships *Beaver, Eleanor* and *Dartmouth* participated in the Boston Tea Party, and sent the ship *United States* to the Falkland Islands to bring back whale oil and seal skins, reviving trade for Nantucket after the Revolutionary War. Later Hong Kong and Shanghai became ports for trade.

In 1712 the sperm whale was found to be a more profitable industry and the whaling industry moved offshore. Captain Chris Hussey having been blown off course, found that the oil from the whale's head was of much higher quality than the right whales. Nantucketers left to search for these whales as far away as the Pacific Ocean, often leaving home for 3-4 years. Tales of the *Essex*, sunk by a whale, inspired Herman Melville to write "Moby Dick", and in 2000 Nathaniel Philbrick to publish "In the Heart of the Sea".

From 1725 on Nantucket was to become America's premier whaling port. By 1730 Nantucket had 25 whalers and over 80 by 1840. However during and after the Revolution the island was to suffer major economic losses since Great Britain refused to trade with the colonies. Nantucket was to rule as the whaling port until well into the 1800s with ships going even further into the Pacific to seek their precious cargo. It was no wonder that the first and most prominent bank on Nantucket was called the Pacific National Bank, a title it still holds today, though now owned by Fleet Boston.

The wharves have been an integral part of Nantucket life. They were home to numerous warehouses, candle factories, rope walks, and shipyards. Straight Wharf was built by Richard Macy in 1723; Old North Wharf in 1774; Old South Wharf (Island Service Wharf) in 1760-62; Swain's Wharf (Commercial Wharf) in 1816 by Zenas Coffin and Sons, and extended in 1831; and Steamboat Wharf (once known as New North Wharf) in 1820. Today the wharves host hundreds of boats and yachtsmen each season, plus quaint cottages and shops. A few fishermen still may try their luck, but it isn't like in the past when you knew the lobster boat had come in. The fishing fleet is almost depleted, and one of the few boats calling Nantucket home is the *Ruthie B*.

The Pacific Club at the end of Main Street was built in 1772 as the counting house for William Rotch and Sons. One room of the building was the first customs house in America from 1783-1913.

The first well was dug in "Sconset in 1776 and the town began to grow, particularly as a "getaway" from Nantucket. "Sconset did not receive any electricity until 1925!!!

Whether one flies or comes by boat to Nantucket you cannot miss its three beacons. Nantucket's most famous lighthouse, Brant Point is on the site of the second oldest lighthouse in the United States, built in 1746. Sankaty Head Lighthouse was built in 1848. Great Point Lighthouse was originally built of wood in 1784 and was called "Sandy Point". The lighthouse burned in 1816 and was rebuilt in 1818. The light was destroyed during a hurricane in 1984, but since then has been rebuilt, much further inland on Great Point. Great Point is a favorite picnic spot, especially at sunset, and offshore bluefish and other fish abound.

The jetty was first proposed to Congress in 1803. The western jetty was built finally in 1881 and the eastern one in 1894. Over 5 thousand tons of stone were brought in by barge. When we were kids we could climb on the rocks, go musseling and walk out as far as the tide would allow us. Today the Jetties are off limits and can be admired, not walked or fished.

The Old Gaol was built in 1805 and is the oldest of its kind in New England. My grandmother had many tales to tell of the jail, and I wish she were here to regale us of the time the jail keeper, having known my grandfather, locked her in the jail as a prank.

Nantucket's African American and Cape Verdean population have influenced the cooking of the island. Such foods as Portuguese bread and Chorizo sausages are on local menus. The first African Americans came to the island as slaves, but slavery was abolished on the island in 1773, ten years before the Commonwealth of Massachusetts abolished slavery. The Cape Verdeans came for the fishing and cranberry industries.

Steamers first began coming to the island in 1818. The Nantucket Steamboat Company was founded in 1832. The first boat was named the *Telegraph* and later renamed the *Nebraska*. The fare, including meals was $2.00. In 1855 the Nantucket & Cape Cod Steamship Company built the steamer, *Island Home*. Until the 1920s the boats were sidewheelers. Today the ferries and fast boats carry passengers and freight to and from the island. Gone are the days when my family had a stateroom and the trip took most of a day. The ferries back then also had dining rooms, not quick snack bars. Even before that my mother remembers coming up from New York on the Fall River Line, an overnight trip to New Bedford and then transferring to the *Nobska*. However, the chowder and hot dogs are still good, and nothing is more pleasant than sitting on the deck, enjoying the view and reading a good book.

Petticoat Row, on Centre Street, received its name because of the manywomen who maintained businesses between 1763 and1855, while their men were off at sea. Most of Centre Street burned during the Great Fire of 1846, but quickly was rebuilt.

Maria Mitchell was the first female astronomer in America. Her father maintained a small observatory atop the Pacific Bank building, where he was a cashier. In 1847 she was the first woman to discover a planet, and in 1848 was the first woman admitted to the American Academy of Arts and Sciences. In addition she was the first professor of astronomy at Vassar College. I doubt she had much time for cooking, but hopefully retreated back to Nantucket for its delicacies.

The "Mirror" was founded in 1845 and merged with the "Inquirer" in 1865. I shall never forget the size of the paper. We often had to stretch out on the floor just to read it. Today, though not quite as large, it is still a local paper filled with interesting island news. For many years the paper announced when families were arriving or departing the island. Today at least they still have a column that recollects what happened 25, 50, 75 and 100 years ago.

The grand mansions built along Main Street were constructed in the 1830s and 1840s. Joseph Starbuck built the "Three Bricks" at a cost of over $40,000. The Hadwen House (1845) at 96 Main Street and the Wright House at 94 Main Street were built by the author's great uncle. Her grandfather was born in 100 Main Street, a house that dates back to the 1700s.

1846 proved to be a disastrous year for much of the historic district, including many of the wharves laden with whale oil, were destroyed by a fire. The Great Fire spread rapidly destroying the Athenuem and 3200 volumes of books and all of Broad Street, except for the Jared Coffin House. After the fire Federal Street was widened and the downtown district rebuilt. The water fight on Main Street during the 4th of July festivities begins with the 1840 Cataract Hand Pumper used during the Great Fire and now owned by the Nantucket Historical Association.

The Atheneum was rebuilt in 1847 and is one of the oldest libraries in continuous service in the United States. The library not only has a large collection of Nantucket books, but scrimshaw, ship models, paintings and historic Nantucket furniture. The Whaling Museum was also built in 1847 by William Hadwen and Nathaniel Barney as a candle factory.

In 1849 over 600 men left the island to join the California Gold Rush. But it was the discovery of oil in Pennsylvania and the refining of oil that led to the demise of Nantucket's whaling industry. The last whaling ship, the bark *Oak* sailed from Nantucket on November 16, 1869, ending Nantucket's very prosperous era. The bar in the harbor blocked larger vessels from entering the harbor. New Bedford had taken over as the leading port in 1825.

The first lightship was placed in service in 1854. *South Shoal* had been a Nantucket whaler, and was the predecessor of the *Nantucket*, now retired. On these lightships men watched over the Nantucket shoals, and during their free time began making the famed Nantucket lightship baskets.

Cranberries were first cultivated on Nantucket in 1857. Prior to 1959 234 acres of bogs were cultivated, the largest contiguous cranberry bog in the world. Now the bogs have been divided up to conserve water. Wooden scoops were originally used to pick the cranberries. Today the bogs are flooded, with the cranberries rising to the surface and pulled to the edge of the bog with wooden booms. They are then washed and loaded on to trucks, and shipped off island. Flying over these bogs in October is just the most incredible sight, seeing the crimson color dotting the island. The bogs are leased to Northland Cranberries, Inc. by the Nantucket Conservation Foundation. A long holiday week-end in October usually is set aside for the Nantucket Harvest and Cranberry Harvest Week-end. Easton Street is named for George Easton who owned a wholesale cranberry business on Nantucket.

The annual fair began in 1856-57. The Nantucket Agricultural Society purchased 10 acres in South Pasture for the fair in 1859. On August 15, 1860 a picnic and clambake was held at the fairgrounds instead of a bicentennial celebration. In 1861 the Coast Guard visited the island and on July 8-9 a large clambake was arranged for them.
The Cliffside Beach Club is located on property that has been a beach club since 1864. The colorful umbrellas and beach chairs present a picture perfect setting. Growing up at my grandparents' house next door we remember when the beaches were private property. Often beachgoers would be kicked off Cliffside, only to end up on ours, and then told they had to go to the Jetties, or another public beach.

The U.S. Life Saving Service Station was built at Surfside in 1874, and was one of the Humane Society stations that rescued shipwrecked and distressed sailors. Today the Nantucket Life Saving Museum preserves some of this history through artifacts, photographs, and paintings. The shoals off Nantucket were notorious for many shipwrecks.

One of the houses (still standing) on Hulbert Avenue in 1899 was built for Henry O. Underwood from Boston, and owner of Underwood's Deviled Ham, which is used in several recipes in this book.

Nantucket has two pharmacies next door to each other on Main Street, with a third outside of town. Not only can you get your prescription, but a real treat is to sit at the old-fashioned soda fountain, eating a grilled cheese or tuna salad sandwich, or savoring one of their ice cream cones. Hard to believe the A&P was once located here, but thank goodness it has survived staying in town, on Lower Main Street.

The Opera House Cup has been around since 1972. The annual event grew from 12 participants to many times that number now. Watching the race from your own or a friend's boat includes a gourmet picnic, and hopefully the weather will cooperate. During the 1991 race Hurricane Bob began to make its appearance, and in 1994 several boats, including *Ticonderoga* were dismasted, a very sorry sight for these elegant, classic boats.

The Daffodil Festival was founded in 1974 when the late Jean MacAusland, publisher of Gourmet Magazine, persuaded the Nantucket Garden Club to invite the American Daffodil Society to sponsor a daffodil show on the island. Since that time over 1 million daffodil bulbs have been planted. In April these brilliantly colored flowers dot every roadway, and a festival with vintage cars, a parade, and picnic is held.


### Historic Inns, Taverns and Clubs

From Nantucket's earliest days the island has always offered hospitality to those visiting, whether whalers, or more recently summer visitors to the resort. Tristam Coffin, one of the original settlers had operated ordinaries (a tavern or eating house that served regular meals) in Salisbury, Massachusetts before settling on the island with his family. Few buildings were known to exist as "hotels". Instead people took in boarders.

For those of you unfamiliar with the term "squantum" this was an outing by boat to a beach where one usually consumed a clambake – chowder, clams, chicken, corn, potatoes, and all the other trappings. A favorite place for a squantum was at Quidnet.

"Shanunga", one of the oldest houses built in "Sconset was once a store, post office and tavern.

The Overlook Hotel on Step Lane was originally called the Veranda House. Part of the house dates to the Gayer House (1684). In 1945 the Overlook was purchased by Mr. and Mrs. Thomas J. Devine. The Indian Room was famous for fried bread dough known as "doughboys".

The Woodbox, a charming inn and restaurant on Fair Street is Nantucket's oldest surviving inn, built in 1709. The house was owned by Daniel, John and Caleb Bunker in 1717. The two buildings were attached in 1931. In 1950 the house was sold to Marie W. F. Tutein. Not long after this, the author's grandmother spent her wedding (second wedding) night at her home around the corner from the Woodbox. Unbeknownst to the bride and groom alarm clocks had been set to go off all night!!!!! However, the bride and groom rallied enough energy to have breakfast at The Woodbox the next morning.

The Chanticleer in "Sconset is one of Nantucket's elegant restaurants. Part of the building dates to c1810. The left side was once a fishing cottage owned by Charles Paddock and was located on the Bluff. Uriah Bunker moved the building in 1836 when New Street was opened.

When whaling became a major industry, establishments blossomed as boarding houses, mainly run by women. 'Sconset became an escape from the bustling town of Nantucket. Some of the early boarding houses were run by Elisha Starbuck; the Federal Street House, by Nathaniel C. Cary; Samuel Cary's house at the corner of Main and Orange Streets. Eliza Ann Barney ran the Gardner House at 69 Main Street with rates of $3 for the week in 1843. The Atlantic House, Main Street, "Sconset was opened in 1848 by Henry S. Crocker, and served dinner.

Seafood houses were to become popular on the wharves. Joseph Winslow opened the "Ship and Whales" in 1826, which also provided lodging. In 1833 James W. Dennison opened a New Hotel providing meals at any hour. In 1833 Jacob Jones opened the Eating House at 5 Whale Street.

The Ship's Inn was built in 1831 as the Captain Obed Starbuck House. Elisha Starbuck and James Athearn opened the Washington House in 1832. The fire of 1836 started in the kitchen of the house and destroyed buildings on Union and Main Street. Many of the historic district's boarding houses and hotels were destroyed during the 1846 fire.

One of Nantucket's favorite inns, The Jared Coffin House, has a long history. The house was built for Jared Coffin in 1845 at Broad and Centre Streets. After the Great Fire of 1846 the house was bought for $7,000 by the Nantucket Steamboat Company. It was then called the Ocean House with Mr. and Mrs. R.F. Parker as proprietors. In 1850 Mr. and Mrs. Parker left the Ocean House and went to the Mitchell House on Union Street. Jervis Robinson took over the Ocean House and allowed no alcohol to be served on its premises.

In 1857 the Ocean House was purchased by Eben W. Allen for $5500. Mr. Allen built the Bathing House on Cliff Shore in 1864. Mr. Allen sold the Ocean House in 1873 to Allen L. Howe and William A. Elmer for $15,000. On August 27, 1874 a dinner was given at Ocean House for President and Mrs. Ulysses S. Grant and General (Secretary of War) and Mrs. Belknap. The menu included cold meats, ham, tongue, chicken, roast beef, lamb, cake, Charlotte Russe, lemon and wine jellies, ice cream and fruit. In 1936 the hotel was sold to John O. Wilsson for $48,000. the Jared Coffin House was conveyed to the Nantucket Historical Trust in 1961 and sold to Philip W. Read for $545,000.

After the Great Fire of 1846 many saloons started serving ice cream, not liquor. The first was opened on Centre Street by Charles L'Hommedieu, and later renamed the Sherburne Saloon. He also opened an ice cream stand in "Sconset on Jefferson Avenue. Thompson's Saloon opened on Main Street in 1848, J.A. Ray's Nauticon Saloon also on Main Street in 1849, and in 1851 L.A. Hooper opened a confectionery and saloon on Centre Street. The Union Store at Main and Centre Streets carried King Arthur Flour and Kennedy's Biscuits.

The Bunker Hill House in "Sconset, owned by Samuel Bunker, was sold to Stephen B. Gibbs in 1852 and used as a billiard saloon. The Cottage Saloon on Main Street opened in 1855 with J.F. Murry as proprietor. Meals, especially seafood, were served, and ladies had a separate entrance. In 1860 the Ice Cream Rooms & Eating Saloon were opened by Mrs. Lydia C. Cottle on Liberty Street. Also that year the Oyster & Ice Cream Saloon run by Mrs. Fish opened on Orange Street. Beginning in 1865 Irene Fisher began taking in boarders and serving meals at 45

Orange Street. Meals cost 50 cents and lodging 25 cents. In 1866 Sara B. Ross opened a Refreshment and Ice Cream Saloon on Orange Street. A year later Mrs. Andrew Winslow opened an Ice Cream Saloon at 22 Orange Street.

During 1872-73 the Ocean View House was built in 'Sconset by Charles H. Robinson and Dr. Franklin A. Ellis.

The Springfield House, now 21 N. Water Street, was purchased for $800 by Almon T. Mowry in 1872. In 1945 the Harbour House was opened made up of the Springfield House (1883), the Dining Room House (1902) and was known as Crest Hall.

The Wauwinet House opened to great fanfare on June 14, 1876, serving clam chowder, lobster and other island delicacies. In 1934 a new Wauwinet House was rebuilt, with the present one in 1988. The area is named for the Indian chief Wauwinet.

During the 1870s and 1880s Nantucket was promoted as a resort. The Ocean House Hotel was listed in R.H. Cook's Tourist Guide in 1871. In 1875 the Inquirer & Mirror began to list hotel arrivals at 6 inns.

In 1881 the first railroad operated from town to Surfside, with service to "Sconset. With the railroads, visitors and residents could head to other parts of the island. A popular destination became Surfside with its beautiful beach. The Surfside Hotel was moved here from Rhode Island in 1883 by Henry and Charles Coffin. The Weeweeder Hotel was built in 1915 by J. Butler Folger. Coatue had its own Cedar House that served meals from 8AM to 11 PM. During the 1920s Tunnington's on Coatue served luncheon, dinner and supper parties.

The Sea Cliff Inn was one of Nantucket's largest hotels with a commanding view of the harbor and Nantucket Sound. The hotel was built in 1887. The hotel sold for $75,000 in 1936 and was closed 1942-43. The inn was sold to Sherburne Associates in 1965 for $65,000. The last season of operation was 1972 with the hotel razed in 1977. Today several private homes occupy the site.

The Folger Hotel property on Easton Street was purchased by Charles Folger from Elijah Alley in 1888. The Point Breeze Hotel opened in 1891 with the pavilion built in 1904. Gordon Folger purchased the property in 1936, and in 1972 the property was sold to Mr. and Mrs.

William Bowman for $250,000. The hotel was sold again several years ago.

During the 1890s a number of hotels were built, including the Nesbitt Cottage on Broad Street, and the Roberts House on Centre Street. During World War II the Nesbitt Inn was used by the Coast Guard for offices and an infirmary. In 1960 the Roberts House became the Bayberry Inn, but was purchased in 1975 by Mr. and Mrs. Michael O'Reilly, and retains its original name. In 1895 the Holiday Inn, previously the American House, opened on Orange Street. Today the property is owned by the author's family as a private home.

The Nantucket Yacht was organized in 1890 as the Nantucket Athletic Club. The clubhouse was built in 1904. The yacht club was incorporated in 1920. Today the yacht club occupies a prime location in downtown Nantucket overlooking the harbor.

In 1897 Thomas Lewis applied to the town for a license for a liquor saloon. His application was turned down. He and Andrew T. Backus were finally able to open one in 1903.

In 1898 the golf club was organized in 'Sconset, and incorporated in 1921. Sankaty Golf Club has a world-renowned course and excellent food, open to members and their guests only.

The Sconset Casino was founded in 1900, mainly as a tennis club. Over the years, plays, movies, dances, and other summer pastimes have taken place here.

The Nantucket Hotel was built on Brant Point in 1906. Some of the houses on Hulbert Avenue and the Dreamland Theater are part of the old structure.

W.H. Sisson held forth on Chestnut Street at "Kenney's Famous Salt Water Taffy", which also sold popcorn.

The Wharf Rat Club, a private club located on Old North Wharf was founded in 1915. The building was originally a general store where men would sit around a pot-bellied stove and tell stories. Even today membership is somewhat based on one's story telling skills.

Anna Ward who had been at the Grill Room in The Ships Inn opened an inn at 94 Main Street to serve "Luncheon, Dinner, and Supper Parties" in

1919. Also in that year $3,000 in wines and liquors were allegedly stolen from the home of actor Robert Hilliard in "Sconset.

The Westmoor Inn on Cliff Road dates from 1917 and was built as a private residence for Wilhelm Voss of New York. The Holdgate family purchased the property in 1953 to use as an inn.

In 1920 the coal schooner *Allen Gurney* was sold to Gladys Wood and Margaret Prentice becoming a tearoom "The Skipper on Steamboat Wharf". This was to become an island favorite, overlooking the harbor, ferries, and selling the finest shore dinners around. Waiting for a meal allowed one to indulge in fresh vegetables and olives, or to be given bread to feed to the seagulls. Sadly the Skipper is long gone, but how we loved our Sunday dinners there.

The White Elephant Hotel was built on property owned by Elizabeth Temple Ludwig in 1920. In 1951 the guest house was sold to Mr. and Mrs. Paul F. Klingelfuss. In 1962 Walter Beinecke razed the hotel. In 1969, 1989, and 2000 the hotel was updated to its present structure overlooking Nantucket harbor. The Breakers became an annex of the White Elephant in 1966.

The Old Pullman Lunch became Allen's Diner in 1921. This had once been the Brill coach of the Nantucket Railroad and ran for the last time in 1917. Today the Club Car has a bar, dining room, and a piano player in the evening.

In 1925 the Chopping Bowl opened on Union Street. The restaurant served refreshments, had dancing, and painting exhibits. The "Iceless Soda Fountain" was installed at the R.G. Coffin drug store on Main Street. On August 8 the Point Breeze Hotel was destroyed by fire, but rebuilt in 1926. The Tavern-on-the-Moors opened in 1927. Lobster dinners were $2.50, shore dinners were lunches $1.00, and dinners $1.50.

In 1937 Leon M. Royal who held the lease for the Cliff Bathing Beach opened the Club Royale serving meals from 11 AM to midnight.

In 1940 the Broadview Hotel property on the Cliff was sold to Grafton Kennedy, the author's grandfather, for $5,000. He had bought the adjacent, "Oversea", in 1933.

The Summer House in "Sconset was once part of the Moby Dick Inn, made up of small cottages and a restaurant, built 1942-43.

Three of the "in places" to go during the 1960s were the pavilion at the Harbour House, the Opera House and the Mad Hatter. Each had a lively bar, dining room, and music in the evening. Sadly all are now gone. The Mad Hatter was torn down recently. The Harbour House building and Opera House are now shops.

## Nantucket Baskets

The history of Nantucket would not be complete without the mention of Nantucket baskets. For more information on the baskets please refer to Katherine and Edgar Seeler's book "Nantucket Lightship Baskets", E. Norman Flayderman's "Scrimshaw and Scrimshanders Whales and Whalemen", or Mary Eliza Starbuck's "My House and I".

The earliest baskets were used to gather fruits, such as blueberries and blackberries; vegetables; eggs; and other foodstuffs; herbs; blankets and clothing. The splint baskets were made by the Indians, originally square on the bottom and later, round. It was known that in 1802 the Mashpee Indians came over from Cape Cod to sell their baskets. Later ladies used the baskets for knitting. The last man with Indian blood to die on the island was Abram Quary in 1842. Some of his baskets can be seen at the Peter Foulger Museum.

The term "lightship basket" refers to the making of the baskets on the *Nantucket South Shoal Lightship* and were well known by 1856. These were made by the men stationed on the lightship to while away many lonely times. The last baskets were made on the lightship in the 1890s.

Today's baskets are woven of rattan, which had originally come from the Pacific, have elaborate lids decorated with ivory in the shape of a whale, seagull, flowers, or almost anything. They are used as pocketbooks; carrying fruits, flowers or vegetables from the morning trucks on Main Street; to holding ornate flower arrangements; or even in the shape of cradles, candle holders, and other uses.

# *Appetizers*

**Sunset at Great Point – A favorite place for appetizers and a BBQ**

# Lobster Rounds

½ stick butter
½ cup Parmesan cheese
1 egg yolk
¼ cup dry Sherry

¼ teaspoon cayenne
1 teaspoon Worcestershire sauce
2 cups lobster meat
French baguette

- Preheat the oven to 400°.
- Slice the bread very thin and place on a cookie sheet. Put in oven 5 minutes to a side, or until just browned.
- In a bowl cream the butter and cheese. Add the egg yolk, Sherry, cayenne and Worcestershire sauce. Gently fold in the lobster.
- Spoon some of the lobster mixture on each slice of bread.
- Bake 5-10 minutes, or until just bubbling.

# Curried Lobster Salad on Corn Fritters

Lobster salad (p. 129)

Corn fritters (p. 115)

- Spoon the lobster salad on the fritters. Place on a platter and garnish with fresh basil.

# Lobster Dip

8 ounces cream cheese
¼ cup mayonnaise
1 clove garlic, minced
2 Tbls. parsley, chopped

½ pound lobster meat
1 Tbls. lemon juice
¼ cup dry Sherry
Dash of cayenne

- Preheat oven to 350°.
- Combine all the ingredients in a small baking dish. Bake 15 minutes or until just warmed. Sprinkle with paprika.
- Serve with crackers or thin sliced French bread.
- This also can be served cold. Just combine ingredients and serve.

# Little Neck Clams

Nantucket has always had a large population from Cape Verde or with Portuguese descent. Chorizo, a type of Portuguese sausage, is found in a number of island dishes.

4 dozen little neck clams
½ stick butter
½ cup white wine
½ pound chorizo, chopped
2 large tomatoes, finely chopped
2 cloves garlic, finely chopped
2 shallots, finely chopped

¼ cup fresh parsley
2 Tbls. basil
1 cup dry bread crumbs
2 teaspoons oregano
¼ cup parmesan cheese
Salt and pepper

- Preheat the oven to 350°.
- Place the clams on a cookie sheet and bake until they just open. Reserve the broth. Remove the clams from the shells and chop finely. Separate the clam shells.
- In a bowl combine the clams and chorizo.
- Melt the butter in a skillet and saute the shallots and garlic. Stir in the bread crumbs, parsley, tomatoes, basil, oregano, cheese and wine.
- Stir in enough of the clam broth to moisten.
- Divide the clams and chorizo among the clam shells. Spoon the bread crumb mixture on top.
- Bake 10 minutes and then brown under the broiler.

# Baked Clams

2 dozen littleneck clams
1 stick butter, melted
1 cup fresh bread crumbs

1 cup onion, chopped fine
¼ cup fresh parsley
¼ teaspoon cayenne

- Preheat oven to 350°.
- Place clams on a cookie sheet and bake until they open. Remove the clams and cool.
- Finely chop the clams. Reserve the clam broth and shells.
- In a bowl combine the clams, butter, onion, parsley, clam broth and cayenne.
- Stuff the clam shells with the clam mixture. Top with the bread crumbs.
- Place under broiler until bubbly.

# Smoked Bluefish Pate

1 pound smoked bluefish
2 scallions
8 ounces cream cheese

Juice of 1 lemon
Fresh dill

- Remove the skin from the fish.
- Place the fish in a food processor and pulse for a short time until broken up. Add scallion, lemon juice and cream cheese.
- Remove from processor and chill overnight. Place in a serving dish and garnish with fresh chopped dill.
- Serve with crackers or thinly sliced French bread.

# Mussels Casino

4 pounds mussels
½ cup dry white wine
½ stick butter
2 shallots, chopped
2 cloves garlic, crushed

½ cup bread crumbs
¼ cup freshly grated parmesan cheese
¼ cup fresh basil leaves

- Scrub the mussels and remove beards. Place in a large pot with the wine. Cover and cook until the mussels have opened. Remove from heat.
- Remove the mussels from the shells and cut into small pieces. Reserve the liquid and one shell from each mussel.
- Melt the butter in a pan and saute the shallots. Add the garlic and bread crumbs. Moisten with remaining liquid. Add mussels.
- Spoon mixture into mussel shells.
- Sprinkle with freshly grated parmesan cheese.
- Broil until the top is just browned.
- Garnish with basil leaves.
- Serve warm or chilled.

# Nantucket Mussels

½ cup olive oil
1 large onion, finely chopped
½ cup pine nuts
2 cups cooked rice
½ cup dried cranberries

½ teaspoon ground cinnamon
1 teaspoon salt
6 dozen mussels with shells
¼ cup white wine

- ♦ In a skillet heat the olive oil and saute the onions until translucent.
- ♦ Add the pine nuts, rice, cranberries, cinnamon and salt.
- ♦ In a large pan heat the wine and add the mussels. Bring to a boil and let steam until mussels are opened. Remove mussels and let cool. Reserve the broth and to rice mixture.
- ♦ Cut one shell off the mussel and top the mussel with a spoonful of the rice mixture.
- ♦ Place mussels on a cookie sheet and put under broiler until just bubbling.
- ♦ Serve hot or chilled.

# Scallops with Dill Sauce

2 pounds bay scallops                ½ cup white wine

- ♦ In a skillet heat the wine and add the scallops. Cook for 5 minutes. Cool.

*Sauce*

1 cup mayonnaise
¼ cup fresh parsley
1 scallion

1 cup fresh spinach
2 Tbls. fresh dill

- ♦ Combine all the sauce ingredients in a food processor.
- ♦ Serve in a bowl as a dip for the scallops.

# Bacon Wrapped Scallops

½ pound bacon
1 pound sea scallops

Toothpicks
Maple syrup

- Preheat oven to 400°.
- Cut the bacon slices into three pieces. Wrap each around a scallop. Secure with a toothpick.
- Pour some maple syrup into a bowl and dip each bacon wrapped scallop in syrup.
- Bake in oven until bacon is crisp, about 15-20 minutes.

# Smoked Scallops with Pesto

2 pounds sea scallops
1 French baguette

Pesto

- Smoke the scallops on a smoker, or grill them.
- Thinly slice the bread. Spread the bread with pesto.
- Top with a scallop.

*Pesto*

1 large bunch basil leaves
½ cup parmesan cheese
¼ cup pine nuts

2 cloves garlic
¼ cup olive oil

- Combine all the ingredients in a food processor until the basil is very finely chopped.

# Codfish Balls with Salsa

1 pound dried codfish
1 medium onion, chopped
4 cups mashed potatoes
4 slices bacon

¼ teaspoon cayenne
Salt and pepper
Butter

- Soak the codfish overnight.
- The next day boil the codfish and drain.
- In a skillet brown the bacon. Remove and add the onions, sauteing until translucent.
- In a bowl combine the codfish, onion, mashed potatoes, bacon, cayenne, salt and pepper.
- Shape into small balls. Melt the butter in the skillet used for the onions and bacon. Brown the codfish balls.
- Serve with tomato salsa (p. 79)
- Larger codfish cakes can be made and served as an entrée.

# Swordfish Blinis

*Blini*

1 cup flour
1 egg
1 cup milk

2 Tbls. sour cream
1 teaspoon baking powder
1 egg

- Combine all ingredients in a bowl.
- Heat the butter in a griddle and drop batter by teaspoonfuls. Turn. Remove from heat and put on a platter.

1 pound swordfish, grilled
½ cup sour cream

2 Tbls. fresh dill, chopped
Fresh dill for garnish

- In a bowl combine the sour cream and chopped dill.
- On each blini place a small piece of the swordfish.
- Top with sour cream and dill. Garnish with a sprig of dill.
- This also is good with grilled or smoked scallops.

# Crab Mold

8 oz. can tomato soup
8 ounces cream cheese
2 Tbls. gelatin dissolved in ½ cup water
½ pound fresh crab meat
½ cup onion, chopped

½ cup celery, chopped
1½ Tbls. horseradish
¼ cup lemon juice
1 cup mayonnaise
Dash of Tabasco

- ◆ In a sauce pan heat the tomato soup. Add the cream cheese until melted, and stir until smooth.
- ◆ Remove from the heat and add remaining ingredients.
- ◆ Pour into a fish mold. Chill. Unmold.
- ◆ Serve with crackers.

# Fried Crab Balls

1 pound crab meat
¼ cup mayonnaise
2 Tbls. bread crumbs

1 egg
½ teaspoon Worcestershire
½ teaspoon Old Bay Seasoning

- ◆ In a bowl combine all the ingredients.
- ◆ Shape into small balls.
- ◆ In a skillet melt butter and gently brown the crab balls.
- ◆ Serve with salsa (p. 79)

# Salmon Blini

1 pound smoked salmon
Blini
1 cup sour cream

1 large bunch dill
1 small jar caviar

- ◆ Make double blini recipe (p. 24)
- ◆ Place the blini on a platter and top each with a piece of salmon, then sour cream, caviar and a sprig of dill.

# Salmon Roll-ups

1 pound thinly sliced smoked
salmon
8 ounces cream cheese
¼ cup fresh dill

2 Tbls. capers
¼ cup red onion, chopped
Juice of 1 lemon

- ◆ In a bowl combine the cream cheese, dill, capers, onion and lemon juice. Spread on the salmon slices.
- ◆ Roll up each salmon slice.
- ◆ Slice across salmon into ½ inch slices.
- ◆ Serve on a platter and garnish with fresh dill.

# Salmon Mousse

1 pkg. gelatin
2 Tbls. lemon juice
¼ cup onion
½ cup boiling water
½ cup mayonnaise

½ teaspoon paprika
1 teaspoon dill
1 pound salmon fillet, no bones
1 cup heavy cream

- ◆ Smoke the salmon on a smoker for 1 hour.
- ◆ In a food processor add gelatin, hot water, and lemon juice. Blend for 30 seconds. Add mayonnaise, paprika, dill, and salmon. Slowly add the cream. Blend 30 seconds.
- ◆ Pour into a fish shaped mold. Refrigerate.
- ◆ Unmold on a fish plate. Garnish with fresh dill.
- ◆ Serve with crackers.
- ◆ This also can be served as a salad on a bed of greens.

# Salmon Canapes

1 baguette
½ pound smoked salmon, cut into 1" pieces
8 ounce pkg. cream cheese

½ cup sour cream
Juice of ½ lemon
¼ cup fresh dill, chopped

- ◆ Cut the baguette into ½" slices and place on a cookie sheet. Place under broiler and toast each side.
- ◆ In a bowl beat together the cream cheese, sour cream and lemon juice. Stir in the dill.
- ◆ Spread each baguette with the dill mixture. Cover with a piece of salmon.
- ◆ Other smoked fish can be substituted for the salmon.

# Seafood Baguettes

2 French bread baguettes
½ pound smoked salmon, cut into 1 inch pieces

1 pound smoked scallops
1 pound medium shrimp

- ◆ Slice the baguettes into ½ inch slices and place on cookie sheet.
- ◆ Spread with pesto and top with the salmon, scallops or shrimp.
- ◆ Place under broiler to just heat.

*Pesto*

2 large bunches basil leaves
½ cup olive oil
4 garlic cloves

½ cup fresh parmesan cheese
¼ cup pine nuts

- ◆ Combine all the ingredients in a food processor until smooth.

# Bruschetta

Bruschetta can be made with a variety of toppings. Tomatoes are the most commonly used, but roasted peppers or other vegetables can add flavor and color to the bread.

1 French bread baguette
4 large tomatoes, finely chopped
¼ cup olive oil
1 large bunch fresh basil,
chopped and stems removed

2 green onions, finely chopped
¼ teaspoon salt
½ teaspoon fresh ground pepper
½ cup freshly grated parmesan cheese

- Thinly slice the baguette.
- In a bowl combine the tomatoes, olive oil, green onion, basil, salt and pepper.
- Spread on the bread slices. Top with parmesan cheese.
- These can be served at room temperature or placed under the broiler until the cheese is just slightly browned.

# Deviled Ham Puffs

8 ounces cream cheese
1 egg yolk, beaten
2 Tbls. onion, chopped
½ teaspoon baking powder

1 teaspoon horseradish
½ teaspoon Tabasco sauce
all bread rounds
2 2 ½-ounce cans deviled ham

- Preheat oven to 375°.
- In a bowl combine the cheese, egg yolk, onion, baking powder, horseradish and Tabasco sauce.
- Place the bread rounds on a cookie sheet and place under broiler until just toasted on one side. Remove from the oven.
- Spread the untoasted side with deviled ham, and cover each with some of the cheese mixture.
- Bake for about 15 minutes, or until puffed and brown.

# Over-Sea Cocktail Special

"Over-Sea" was the name of my grandparent's house on The Cliff. They entertained a lot, and always had two old-fashions before dinner. The front porch of the house was an inviting place to watch the boats coming in from a race, or the ferries. When anyone departed from the island by the ferry, everyone would race back from the ferry dock and wave a sheet in farewell. Always a sad time, but throwing two pennies overboard meant a return trip.

½ pound sharp cheddar cheese
2 ½ cups flour
2 sticks butter

1 cup pecans
1 teaspoon cayenne

- ◆ Combine all the ingredients in a food processor until a ball is formed. Remove from processor.
- ◆ Form a roll similar to ice-box cookies. Wrap in foil.
- ◆ Store in refrigerator at least 24 hours before using.
- ◆ When ready to use, slice into thin discs, and heat in 300° oven for 10 minutes.

# Gagi's Stuff & Nonsense

½ box Cherrios
½ box Rice Chex
½ box bite-size Shredded Wheat
1 box pretzel sticks
1 large can mixed nuts
¼ cup butter

1 teaspoon celery salt
1 Tbls. garlic powder
1 teaspoon chili powder
1 Tbls. Tabasco sauce
2 Tbls. Worcestershire sauce
1 Tbls. peanut butter

- ◆ Preheat oven to 200°.
- ◆ In a bowl combine the celery salt, garlic powder, and chili powder.
- ◆ In a large roasting pan combine the peanut butter, Worcestershire sauce, Tabasco sauce, and butter. Place in oven until butter is melted. Remove from oven.
- ◆ Add spice mixture, and then cereals, nuts, and pretzels. Combine all ingredients thoroughly.
- ◆ Bake for 1¼ hours in oven.

# Big Ga's Deviled Eggs

12 eggs
1 large can deviled ham
2 Tbls. mustard

1 Tbls. vinegar
¼ cup mayonnaise

- In a large pan bring the eggs to boil, and cook for 10 minutes. Let cool. Shell and slice in half lengthwise. Separate yolks and whites.
- In a bowl combine the egg yolks, mustard, vinegar, ham, and mayonnaise, adding more mayonnaise if too thick.
- Stuff the eggs with yolk mixture.
- Serve on a platter garnished with parsley.

# Cheese Puffs

2 cups flour
1 tablespoon baking powder
¾ cup half and half
6 tablespoons butter

½ teaspoon salt
1 pound fresh sausage
1 cup sharp cheddar cheese

- In a skillet just slightly brown the sausage. Remove and drain.
- Place all ingredients in a food processor and combine thoroughly.
- Form into small balls.
- Bake at 350° for 20 minutes or until golden brown.

# Raspberry Brie

1 pound brie round
1 pint fresh raspberries

2 pkgs. refrigerator crescent rolls
2 Tbls. butter

- Preheat oven to 425°.
- Roll out the rolls on a cutting board. Place in a pie plate.
- Place the cheese in the dough. Top with raspberries. Enclose the cheese with the dough and seal edges. Top with butter.
- Bake 10 minutes or until pastry is golden brown.
- Serve with crackers, or French bread.

# Hot Brie and Cranberries

1 pound round brie
½ cup fresh cranberries
¼ cup brown sugar

1 package crescent rolls
2 Tbls. butter

- ◆ Preheat oven to 425°.
- ◆ Roll out the rolls on a cutting board. Place in a pie plate.
- ◆ Place the cheese in the dough. Top with cranberries and brown sugar. Enclose the cheese with the dough and seal. Top with butter.
- ◆ Bake 10 minutes or until pastry is golden brown.
- ◆ Serve with crackers.

# Cranberry Chutney Brie

1 small round brie
1 package crescent rolls

½ cup cranberry chutney
2 tbls. butter

- ◆ Preheat oven to 425°.
- ◆ Roll out the rolls on a cutting board. Place in a pie plate.
- ◆ Place the cheese in the dough. Top with chutney. Enclose the cheese with the dough and seal. Top with butter.
- ◆ Bake 10 minutes or until pastry is golden brown.
- ◆ Serve with crackers

# Brie and Blue Cheese

1 large round brie
1 pound blue cheese

1 pint raspberries

- ◆ Slice the brie in half through the center.
- ◆ Spread the blue cheese on the bottom layer.
- ◆ Top with other half of brie. Garnish with raspberries.
- ◆ Serve with crackers.

# Pears with Stilton

6 ripe pears                    ½ pound Stilton cheese
Juice of 1 lemon

♦ Thinly slice the pears and put in a bowl of water with the lemon juice.
♦ Remove slices from water and neatly form a circle on a serving platter.
♦ Slice the Stilton into thin slices. Place Stilton on each pear slice.
♦ Blue cheese, camembert or brie can be substituted for the Stilton.

# Fondue

When we were growing up this was a favorite for a cold winter's night. At the time of my wedding many years ago fondue pots were very in as a wedding present. I still have mine after almost 30 years.

Serves 6

½ pound Emmenthaler cheese     ½ cup kirsch
½ pound Gruyere                Salt and pepper
1 clove garlic, minced         ¼ teaspoon fresh grated nutmeg
½ cup dry white wine           1 loaf French bread, cubed

♦ Rub the inside of the fondue pot with the garlic. Add the wine and stir over low heat until boiling.
♦ Slowly add the cheese and stir until melted. Add the other ingredients, except for the bread.
♦ Serve the bread on skewers that can be dipped in the fondue pot.

# Smoked Duck with Black Bean Salsa

1 smoked duck

- ♦ Smoke duck on smoker, or purchase already smoked.
- ♦ Thinly slice the duck.

*Black Bean, Tomato and Avocado Salsa*

1 pound black beans
2 large tomatoes, finely chopped
2 ripe avocados, peeled, seeded and finely chopped
2 green onions, chopped
¼ cup cilantro, chopped

4 jalapeno peppers, seeded and finely chopped
2 Tbls. olive oil
2 cloves garlic, minced
1 Tbls. fresh ground pepper
1 teaspoon kosher salt
2 Tbls. vinegar

- ♦ Soak the beans in water to cover overnight.
- ♦ In a pan bring the water and beans to a boil. Cook until tender. Drain.
- ♦ In a bowl combine all the ingredients.
- ♦ Serve with the duck.

# Pate

1 pound chicken livers
1 stick butter
5 large mushrooms, sliced
Salt and pepper

2 green onions
¼ teaspoon ground cloves
½ teaspoon dry mustard
¼ cup cognac

- ♦ In a skillet saute the chicken livers and mushrooms in ¼ stick butter. Season with salt and pepper. Place in food processor with green onions and blend until smooth. Add rest of ingredients.
- ♦ Remove from food processor and pack in glass loaf pan.
- ♦ Refrigerate at least two hours. Unmold. Place on serving platter.
- ♦ Garnish with nutmeg. Serve with toasted sliced baguette.

# Pate with Walnuts

1 pound chicken livers
1 stick butter
1 cup walnuts or pecans
Salt and pepper

2 Tbls. fresh tarragon
2 Tbls. fresh parsley
¼ cup cognac

- In a skillet saute the chicken livers in ¼ stick butter. Season with salt and pepper. Place in food processor with rest of ingredients. Blend until smooth.
- Remove from food processor and place in glass loaf pan. Refrigerate at least two hours. Unmold and place on a serving platter.
- Garnish with fresh tarragon and parsley. Serve with toasted sliced baguette.

# Chicken Pate

2 cups cooked chicken
1 stick butter, melted
2 Tbls. Port
2 garlic cloves

¼ teaspoon nutmeg
¼ teaspoon allspice
Salt and pepper
Toasted baguette, sliced

- In a food processor combine all ingredients, except bread.
- Remove and pack into a bowl. Serve with bread.

# Baby Spinach Fingers

1 large container boursin cheese
1 pound fresh baby spinach

French bread baguette, sliced

- Put a small spoonful of boursin on each spinach leaf and wrap leaf around cheese.
- Serve each on a slice of bread.

# Spinach Cheesecake

*Crust*

½ cup pine nuts
1 cup fine Italian bread crumbs

½ stick butter, softened

- ◆ Preheat oven to 350°.
- ◆ In a spring form pan combine the ingredients and press into the sides of the pan.
- ◆ Bake for 10 minutes. Cool.

*Filling*

16 ounces cream cheese
3 large eggs
1 pound fresh spinach
2 garlic cloves, crushed

2 Tbls. flour
¼ cup fresh dill
2 large tomatoes sliced

- ◆ In a bowl combine the cream cheese, eggs, spinach, garlic, flour and dill.
- ◆ Arrange the tomatoes in the pine nut crust.
- ◆ Top with spinach mixture.
- ◆ Bake for 50 minutes.
- ◆ Garnish with fresh dill and tomato slices.

# Spinach Dip

2 cups mayonnaise
1 tablespoon dried onion
¼ teaspoon pepper

1 pound fresh spinach
½ jar mango chutney

- ◆ Cook spinach in boiling water until just tender. Drain.
- ◆ Combine all the ingredients in a food processor until thoroughly blended. Place in a serving dish.
- ◆ Serve with crackers or French bread.
- ◆ 1 teaspoon curry or fresh dill can be added for more flavor.

# Mushroom Toasts

8 ounces cream cheese
½ pound mushrooms, chopped
½ stick butter
2 green onions, chopped

¼ teaspoon nutmeg
2 Tbls. Cognac
French bread, thinly sliced

- ◆ Preheat oven broiler.
- ◆ In a skillet saute the mushrooms in the butter.
- ◆ Add the cream cheese, green onions, nutmeg and Cognac.
- ◆ Place the bread on a cookie sheet and top each slice with the mushroom mixture.
- ◆ Place under broiler until just bubbling. Serve immediately.


# Vegetable Cheesecake

8 ounces cream cheese
1 stick butter, softened
½ pound Monterey Jack cheese
with jalapenos, sliced
2 large tomatoes, finely chopped
1 red bell pepper, finely chopped

1 yellow squash or zucchini,
finely chopped
¼ cup fresh basil
2 cloves garlic, minced
¼ cup pine nuts
Salt and pepper

- ◆ Line a 5" x 9" inch pan with plastic wrap. Using some of the basil leaves, line the bowl.
- ◆ In a bowl combine the cream cheese, butter and Monterey Jack cheese. Use ½ of this mixture to line the pan.
- ◆ In a separate bowl combine the tomatoes, pepper, squash, garlic, pine nuts, basil, salt and pepper. Spread over cream cheese layer.
- ◆ Top with remaining cream cheese mixture.
- ◆ Place a damp piece of cheesecloth over the bowl. Cover with plastic wrap. Weight down with a pan.
- ◆ Chill overnight.
- ◆ Remove the plastic wrap and cheesecloth and invert cheesecake onto a serving plate, removing remaining plastic wrap.
- ◆ Serve with crackers or sliced French bread.

# Asparagus Wrapped in Prosciutto

1 pound thin asparagus         1 pound sliced prosciutto

- Remove ends of asparagus stalks.
- Bring 1 cup water to boil in a skillet.
- Boil asparagus for 3 minutes. Remove and cool. The asparagus can also be steamed for 3 minutes.
- Wrap each asparagus stalk with a prosciutto slice.
- Serve on a platter and garnish with fresh dill.
- The asparagus also can be roasted in a 400° oven for 25 minutes.

# Baba Ghannouj

1 medium eggplant        1 teaspoon salt
¼ cup fresh lemon juice        1 Tbls. olive oil
3 cloves garlic, minced        2 Tbls. fresh parsley
1 cup tahina paste        ¼ cup onions, finely chopped

- Preheat oven to 400°.
- Prick the eggplant with a fork in several places. Place the eggplant on a cookie sheet and bake in oven for 30 minutes. Remove and let cool.
- Peel off the skin and cut eggplant into cubes.
- Place in food processor with lemon juice, garlic, tahina paste, and salt until smooth.
- Serve in a bowl and garnish with olive oil, parsley and onions.
- Serve with fresh or toasted pita bread.

# Crudités

1 pound thin asparagus
1 head cauliflower
1 pound broccoli
1 yellow pepper, sliced
1 red pepper, sliced

1 pound cherry tomatoes
1 package radishes
½ pound snow peas
½ pound green beans

- ◆ Arrange the vegetables on a large platter.
- ◆ Serve with one of the dips listed below.

## Ginger Dip

1 cup mayonnaise
1 cup sour cream
1 Tbls. soy sauce

1 can chopped water chestnuts
¼ cup crystallized ginger
2 Tbls. fresh cilantro

- ◆ In a food processor combine all the ingredients. Serve in a bowl with the vegetables.

## Herb Dip

1 cup mayonnaise
1 cup sour cream
¼ cup fresh parsley, chopped
¼ cup chives, chopped

2 cloves garlic, minced
1 Tbls. lemon juice
2 Tbls. tarragon vinegar

- ◆ In a food processor combine all the ingredients. Serve in a bowl with the vegetables.

## Spinach Dip

1 pound fresh spinach
¼ cup pine nuts
2 cloves garlic

8 ounces cream cheese
Juice of 1 lemon
Salt and pepper

- ◆ Combine all the ingredients in a food processor.
- ◆ Serve in a bowl with the vegetables.

# Hummus

Don't do what I did the first time I ever made this. I found what I thought was a perfect recipe. However it called for 6 cloves of garlic. After the first bite I had to throw it out. Too much garlic. Garlic might be good for you, but not that much. I think ended up using 3 cloves of garlic instead.

1 can chick peas, drained
¼ cup parsley
¼ cup onions

¼ cup fresh lemon juice
2 cloves garlic
½ teaspoon salt

- Place all the ingredients in a food processor until smooth.
- Serve with pita bread or toasted pita bread.

*Toasted Pita Bread*

- Preheat oven to 400°.
- Cut the pita bread into 1 inch slices or wedges, and place on cookie sheet.
- Bake for 15 minutes, or until very crispy.

# Spiced Nuts

1 pound shelled walnuts or pecans
½ stick butter, melted

2 Tbls. Worcestershire sauce
2 teaspoons garlic salt
¼ teaspoon cayenne

- Preheat the oven to 300°.
- Combine all ingredients except nuts in a bowl. Add nuts and coat well.
- Place on a cookie sheet and bake for 15-20 minutes. Please watch carefully as they brown very quickly.

# Drinks

**Nantucket Vineyards**

In 1873 the bark *Minmanueth* went aground near Miacomet pond carrying 4,000 bags of coffee, much of which was rescued for the islanders.

William J. Flagg who built "Flaggship" in 'Sconset and once owned the Bluff, also owned a 10,000 acre vineyard along the Ohio River. Among his pastimes was publishing books on European vineyards.

Nantucket Nectars, Nantucket Vineyards and the Cisco Brewery produce Nantucket's own favorite drinks.

# Nantucket Wine Cooler

Dry white wine                                Club soda

- In a wine glass with just a little ice add equal parts of dry white wine and club soda.
- Serve with a lemon or lime slice.

# Cranberry Cooler

For one drink

1½ ounces Bourbon                      1 teaspoon sugar
1½ ounces cranberry juice            2 ice cubes
1 ounce lime juice

- Combine all ingredients in a blender with ice cubes.
- Serve in a tall glass.

# Cranberry Cocktail

2 quarts cranberry juice
2 quarts orange juice

2 cups Grand Marnier
1 cup vodka

- ◆ Combine all ingredients in a punch bowl.
- ◆ Place a round of ice in bowl.
- ◆ Garnish with orange slices.

# Cranberry Apple Punch

1 gallon apple cider
3 quarts cranberry juice
6 cinnamon sticks

2 teaspoons whole cloves
1 orange, thinly sliced with a clove in each orange slice

- ◆ In a large pot heat all the ingredients except orange slices. Bring to a boil and let simmer 15 minutes.
- ◆ Pour into a punch bowl. Garnish with orange slices.

# Cranberry Punch

Serves 16 in punch cups

1 quart cranberry juice
2 cups water
1 cup orange juice
¼ cup lemon juice

1 quart ginger ale
½ cup sugar
½ cup fresh cranberries
1 orange, sliced

- ◆ Combine all ingredients in a punchbowl with an ice ring.

# Hot Spiced Cranberry Punch

Serves 36

1 gallon apple cider
1 gallon cranberry juice
12 cloves
4 sticks cinnamon

12 whole allspice
½ cup brown sugar
Cranberries for garnish

♦ Combine all ingredients in a large pot. Bring to a boil.
♦ Serve hot in a punchbowl. Garnish with fresh cranberries.

# Cranberry Delight

Serves 20

1 gallon cranberry juice
1 bottle club soda
½ teaspoon angostura bitters

1 lime, sliced thinly
Ice ring

♦ Stir the cranberry juice, club soda and bitters in a punch bowl. Add the ice ring.
♦ Garnish with lime slices.

# Mrs. Chase's Rum Punch

2 cups sugar
4 cups water
½ cup orange juice

½ cup fresh lemon juice
½ cup strong tea
½ cup rum

♦ Combine the sugar and water in a sauce pan and bring to a boil.
♦ Combine the orange juice, lemon juice and tea. Add to sugar syrup.
♦ Place in freezer and let turn to mush. Add rum.
♦ Stir a little and let freeze.
♦ Serve in individual glasses with mint.

# Champagne Punch

Serves 16

1 6 ounce can frozen lemonade
1 6 ounce can water
1 cup apricot brandy
1 cup Curacao

2 cups cognac
2 bottles of champagne, chilled
Ice ring

- In a punchbowl combine the lemonade, water, brandy, Curacao and cognac.
- Put the ice ring in the bowl and add the champagne.
- Serve in punch cups.

# Eggnog

1 cup sugar
12 eggs, separated
4 cups milk
4 cups heavy cream

1 cup bourbon
1 cup cognac
Nutmeg

- Beat the egg yolks in a bowl and add ½ cup sugar.
- In another bowl beat the egg whites until stiff and add ½ cup sugar.
- Fold the egg whites into the yolk mixture.
- Fold in the cream and milk.
- Slowly add the Bourbon and Cognac.
- Serve in a punch bowl with freshly grated nutmeg.

# Lemonade

For one drink

2 Tbls. fresh lemon juice
Club soda

Ice
Lemon slice

- Pour lemon juice into glass with ice.
- Fill to top with club soda. Garnish with lemon slice.

# Fish House Punch

*Fourth of July is a perfect time to serve Fish House Punch.*

*Fish House Punch was concocted at the Fish House Club in Philadelphia c1732. This rum punch was to become a favorite for parties and clubs.*

1½ cups sugar  
7 cups tea  
3 cups lemon juice  
1 bottle dark rum  

1 bottle light rum  
1 bottle Cognac  
½ cup peach brandy  

- ◆ Combine the sugar and tea in a punchbowl and stir to dissolve sugar. Add the other ingredients.
- ◆ Let stand for 2 hours, at least, with an ice ring in the bowl.
- ◆ Lemon slices with cloves or strawberries can be used to garnish the punch.
- ◆ Serve in punch cups.

# Iced Tea

Serves 12

12 cups English Breakfast tea  
1 can lemonade concentrate  
1 can grape juice  

1 lime, sliced thinly  
Ice  

- ◆ In a large pitcher combine the tea lemonade and grape juice.
- ◆ Serve in tall glasses with ice and garnish with a slice of lemon.

# Planters' Punch

1 bottle dark rum
1 quart orange juice
1 quart pineapple juice

½ cup lime juice
Lemon or lime slices
Maraschino cherries

- In a pitcher or punchbowl combine the rum and juices.
- Pour into glasses with ice. Garnish with the lime slices and cherries.

# Kir

Kir is such a refreshing drink.

Crème de Cassis
Dry white wine

- Into each glass of dry white wine add a dash of crème de cassis.

# Fruit Punch

2 quarts unsweetened pineapple
juice
Juice of 8 oranges
Juice of 8 lemons

2 cups sugar
4 quarts ginger ale
2 quarts club soda
1 quart strawberries

- In a punch bowl combine the juices with the sugar. Refrigerate.
- Just before serving add ginger ale and club soda.
- Garnish with the strawberries.
- To add real bite, add 1 bottle of dark rum.

*Now Let Us Praise Fried Pies*

# Little Ga's Fruit Punch

Serves 50

3 ½ cups sugar
1 cup fresh lemon juice
1 cup orange juice
1 pint grape juice

1 pint very strong tea
7 quarts water
Orange slices, lemon slices
Ice ring

- In a large punchbowl combine the sugar, lemon juice, grape juice, tea and water.
- Add ice ring and fruit.
- Serve in punch cups.

# Party Punch

4 quarts water
3 cups sugar
12 ounce can frozen lemon juice
1 quart apple juice

2 quarts cranberry juice
1 quart orange juice
1 pint strong black tea

- In a sauce pan bring the water and sugar to a boil. Remove from heat and add rest of ingredients. Mix well. Chill.
- Pour into punch bowl.
- Garnish with lemon and orange slices.

# Mulled Cider Punch

1 gallon cider
4 oranges
Cloves

¼ cup honey
4 cups bourbon

- In a large pot combine the cider and honey.
- Stud the oranges with cloves and add to cider. Bring to a boil. Remove from heat. Add the bourbon.
- Serve in punch cups or mugs.
- Rum can be substituted for the bourbon.

# Old-Fashioned

Every night before dinner my Kennedy grandparents each had two old fashioneds. My grandmother always complained about her weight and how she couldn't drink water or wine with dinner. Did she ever think about the sugar in her old fashioned?

Serves 1 drink

1 teaspoon sugar
¼ teaspoon angostura bitters

1 Tbls. water
2 ounces Bourbon

♦ In a glass combine the ingredients. Add ice cubes. Serve with a cherry and orange slice.

# Manhattans

These were a favorite of Cousin Marge Swain who lived at the Barnacle and on Orange Street.

2 ounces bourbon
½ ounce sweet Vermouth

½ ounce dry Vermouth
Dash of bitters

♦ Stir bourbon and Vermouths well with ice and strain.
♦ Add a cherry, lemon peel, or slice of orange.

# Strawberry Daiquiri

Serves 4

1 six ounce can frozen limeade concentrate
1 quart strawberries

1 cup rum
8 (or more) ice cubes

♦ Place all ingredients in blender.
♦ Serve immediately, or store in refrigerator until ready to use.

# Soups

**Brant Point Lighthouse and Coast Guard Station**

# Clam Chowder

Serve the chowder with Portuguese or sourdough bread and a green salad.

Serves 8

3 dozen quahogs
2 quarts half and half
1 large onion, chopped
8 slices bacon
½ teaspoon pepper

½ teaspoon salt
4 cups diced potatoes
½ stick butter
¼ cup fresh dill

- Preheat oven to 350°.
- Place clams on cookie sheet. Bake until clams just open. Remove the clams from their shells. Reserve the clam broth and put the clams in a large pot.
- Fry bacon in a skillet. Remove bacon and saute onions in bacon fat.
- Boil potatoes until tender.
- To the clam pot add the potatoes, onions, half and half, clam broth, dill, salt and pepper, and last the bacon.
- Simmer until warm, but do not let boil. Just before serving add butter. Serve in bowls and garnish with fresh dill.
- One large leek, chopped, can be substituted for the onion.

# Tomato Lobster Bisque

Serves 4

2 cups cream
4 large tomatoes, chopped
1 pound lobster meat
½ cup celery, diced

¼ cup sherry
2 Tbls. parsley, chopped
2 Tbls. lemon juice

- In a saucepan combine all the ingredients, except lobster and parsley.
- Combine in a food processor and blend until smooth.
- Pour into a soup tureen.
- Gently fold in the lobster meat. Garnish with parsley.
- This can be rewarmed in the sauce pan or served chilled.

# Lobster Bisque

Serves 6

1 small onion
1 carrot
1 stalk celery
1 leek
2 1½ pound lobsters
1 cup white wine

¼ cup cognac
1 quart fish stock
Salt and Pepper
1 cup heavy cream
¼ cup butter
¼ teaspoon cayenne

- Julienne the carrots, celery, onion and leek. Saute in olive oil in a large pot for 2-3 minutes.
- Add the lobsters which have been halved. Cook until the lobsters turn red.
- Add the wine and cognac. Simmer for 5 minutes.
- Remove the lobsters from the pan. Remove the meat from the lobsters.
- Put the shells through a grinder and add back into the pot. Remove the pan from the heat and strain through a sieve, and put liquid back into the pan.
- Add the fish stock. Reheat.
- Add the cream, butter, cayenne and lobster meat.
- Serve in bowls and garnish with fresh parsley.

# Lobster Stew (Easy Lobster Bisque)

Serves 6

½ stick butter
1 pound lobster meat
2 Tbls. flour
6 cups half and half
½ teaspoon salt

½ teaspoon paprika
Dash of cayenne
¼ cup Sherry
Parsley or fresh dill

- Melt the butter in a sauce pan and add flour, making a roux.
- Stir in half and half, salt, paprika, cayenne and Sherry until slightly thickened.
- Gently fold in lobster meat. Serve hot garnished with parsley or dill.

# Bouillabaisse

Serves 12 or more

| | |
|---|---|
| 2 pounds fish heads and bones | 3 tomatoes, peeled and chopped |
| 2 pounds filet of sole or flounder | ½ cup olive oil |
| 1 pound red snapper | 1 ½ cups celery, chopped |
| 4 1½ pound lobsters | ½ cup fresh parsley, chopped |
| 3 dozen mussels | 4 cups fish stock |
| 1 pound scallops | Salt and pepper |
| 2 leeks, chopped | ½ teaspoon cayenne |
| 2 large onions, chopped | 1 cup white wine |
| 4 cloves garlic, minced | |

- ◆ For the fish stock place the fish heads and bones in 2 quarts water in a heavy kettle. Bring to a boil and simmer for 30 minutes.
- ◆ Remove from heat and strain through a sieve or cheesecloth, saving stock.
- ◆ Cut the fish into bite size pieces.
- ◆ Separate the lobster tail and claws, and discard the body. Thoroughly wash the mussels and scallops.
- ◆ Using the kettle, heat the olive oil and add the onions, leeks, celery and garlic. Cook until just brown. Add the parsley, tomatoes, fish stock and white wine. Season with salt, pepper and cayenne. Bring to a boil.
- ◆ Put in the lobsters, mussels and scallops. Cover and simmer for 30 minutes. Add the filet of sole and red snapper. Bring to a boil.
- ◆ Spoon the bouillabaisse into bowls and serve with Portuguese bread and a salad.

# Fish Chowder

Serves 8

4 pounds flounder
½ pound bacon
1 large onion, chopped
2 cloves garlic, minced
4 large potatoes, peeled and
diced

2 quarts half and half
½ stick butter
Salt and pepper
1 teaspoon thyme

- ◆ Cut the bacon into small pieces and place in large kettle. Brown bacon, and add onion, then garlic.
- ◆ Cut the fish into small pieces.
- ◆ In another pot cook the potatoes in boiling water until tender.
- ◆ Add the potatoes to bacon and onions.
- ◆ Add fish, half and half, salt, pepper and thyme. Bring to a boil. Add butter.
- ◆ Serve in bowls. Garnish with snipped dill or parsley.

# Oyster Stew

Serves 6

1 quart oysters
3 green onions, sliced
½ stick butter
6 cups half and half

Salt and pepper
Fresh parsley
Paprika

- ◆ In a sauce pan melt the butter and saute the green onions.
- ◆ Cook the oysters in their liquor for about 5 minutes. Add the green onion, half and half, salt and pepper.
- ◆ Pour into a soup tureen and garnish with paprika and parsley.
- ◆ Serve immediately.

# Scallop Stew

Serves 6

½ stick butter                                    2 pounds sea scallops
½ cup flour                                       ½ cup Sherry
6 cups half and half                              Paprika
½ teaspoon salt                                   Fresh Dill
¼ teaspoon fresh ground pepper

- ♦ Melt the butter in a sauce pan and add the flour.
- ♦ Stir in the half and half, salt, pepper and Sherry.
- ♦ Gently fold in the scallops and simmer for 5 minutes.
- ♦ Pour into a soup tureen and garnish with paprika and fresh dill.

# Gazpacho

Serves 6

1 cucumber, sliced                                5 ripe tomatoes
4 scallions, sliced                               2 Tbls. olive oil
2 carrots, sliced                                 1 teaspoon Worcestershire sauce
4 cloves garlic                                   ¼ teaspoon cayenne
1 green pepper, sliced                            1 cup French bread crumbs

- ♦ Place all the ingredients in a food processor, until just small chunks of the vegetables remain.
- ♦ Pour into a soup tureen.
- ♦ Garnish with chopped pepper, croutons, chopped cucumber, and sour cream.

# Corn Chowder

Serves 4

½ stick butter
1 onion, chopped
4 cups corn
2 scallions, chopped
1 green pepper, chopped

2 cups milk
1 cup cream
Pinch of cayenne
½ pound sharp cheddar cheese
Salt and pepper

- ◆ In a large sauce pan melt the butter. Saute onions until transparent.
- ◆ Add corn, scallions, green pepper, milk, cream, cayenne, cheese, salt and pepper. Bring to a boil. Simmer for 5 minutes.
- ◆ Serve in bowls.
- ◆ 2 cups crab meat, lobster, or scallops can be added to this for a heartier meal.

# Carrot Soup

Serves 4-6

½ stick butter
2 leeks, sliced
1 pound carrots, sliced
4 cups chicken stock

1 cup cream
Salt and pepper
1 Tbls. cilantro

- ◆ In a large saucepan melt the butter. Add the leeks and carrots and saute until tender.
- ◆ Pour in the stock. Add the salt and pepper. Simmer for 20 minutes. Cool.
- ◆ Pour into a food processor and blend until smooth.
- ◆ Return to pan and add cream.
- ◆ This is also very good served chilled.
- ◆ Garnish with fresh cilantro.
- ◆ 1 teaspoon curry powder or ground ginger can be added for more flavor.

# Snap Pea Soup

Serves 4

1 lb. snap peas, string removed
½ cup water
2 large leeks, chopped
4 cups heavy cream
2 mint leaves

Salt and pepper
2 Tbls fresh parsley
¼ cup celery chopped
¼ cup fresh basil

- Combine the peas and the water in a sauce pan and bring to a boil.
- Remove from heat and pour into a food processor. Add other ingredients.
- Serve hot or chilled, garnished with fresh parsley or basil leaves.

# Potato and Ham Soup

Serves 4

1 large onion, chopped
2 leeks, chopped
½ stick butter
2 cups half and half
1 cup chicken stock
4 large potatoes, peeled and cut into small cubes

2 cups cubed ham
½ teaspoon pepper
1 teaspoon salt
2 Tbls. fresh parsley
2 Tbls. fresh dill

- In a large pot melt the butter and saute the leeks and onion.
- Add the potatoes and chicken stock. Cover and cook for 25 minutes or until the potatoes are tender.
- Add the ham, salt, pepper, parsley, dill and half and half. Bring to a boil.
- Serve hot.

# Potato, Garlic and Leek Soup

Serves 4

4 large potatoes, peeled and diced
4 cloves garlic, minced
2 large leeks, chopped
4 slices bacon

1 quart chicken stock
¾ cup sour cream
¼ teaspoon cayenne
Salt and pepper, to taste

- In a large pot brown the bacon and add the garlic. Add the leeks and cook until soft. Add the chicken stock and potatoes. Cook 30 minutes.
- Remove from heat and allow to cool.
- Place in a food processor and add sour cream, cayenne and salt and pepper.
- This can be served hot or chilled.

# Pumpkin Soup

½ stick butter
1 onion, chopped
1 Tbls flour
1 clove garlic, crushed
¼ teaspoon nutmeg

½ teaspoon cinnamon
1 teaspoon brown sugar
¼ cup orange juice
2 cups pumpkin
2 ½ cups chicken stock

- Melt the butter in a large sauce pan and add onions. Cook until transparent.
- Stir in the flour, nutmeg, cinnamon and pumpkin. Cover and simmer for 5 minutes.
- Add the chicken stock, brown sugar and orange juice. Bring to a boil. Simmer for 5 minutes.
- Pour into a food processor until blended.
- Serve hot or chilled with freshly grated nutmeg.

# Curried Butternut Squash Soup

½ stick butter
2 cups onions, chopped
4 teaspoons curry powder
3 pounds butternut squash

2 granny smith apples, peeled, cored, and sliced
3 cups chicken stock
1 cup apple juice

- ♦ Melt the butter in a large pot and add onions and curry until onions are tender.
- ♦ Peel and chop the squash.
- ♦ Add chicken stock, squash and apples to onions and simmer for 25 minutes.
- ♦ Place in food processor and blend until smooth.
- ♦ Return soup to the pot and add apple juice. Simmer.
- ♦ Serve warm in bowls, garnished with apple slices.


# Harvest Squash Soup

Serves 4-6

6 cups squash
2 large leeks, sliced
2 Tbls. butter
2 Tbls. olive oil
3 cups chicken broth

1 cup heavy cream
2 cloves garlic, minced
½ cup brown sugar
1 teaspoon thyme

- ♦ Heat the butter and oil in a large skillet. Add the leeks and garlic.
- ♦ Stir in the squash, brown sugar, thyme, and chicken broth and simmer for 15 minutes. Cool slightly.
- ♦ Pour into a food processor or blender. Blend until smooth.
- ♦ Pour into a soup tureen and stir in cream. Refrigerate until well chilled. Serve chilled, or can be warmed up.

# Fruit Soup

This soup is a delicious starter for a hot night.

Serves 8

1 cantaloupe
1 quart fresh strawberries
without stems
½ pound grapes, no stems
4 apples, peeled, cored and
sliced

1 cup fresh lemon juice
½ cup sugar
2 cups orange juice
5 cups water

- ◆ Cut the cantaloupe in half and discard seeds. Scoop out pulp with a melon baller.
- ◆ In a large pot combine all the ingredients and bring to a boil. Simmer for 15 minutes.
- ◆ Pour into a food processor and puree.
- ◆ Place in a soup tureen and refrigerate for at least two hours.
- ◆ Garnish with mint leaves.
- ◆ Sour cream can also be served with this soup.

# Cucumber Dill Soup

Serves 4

2 cucumbers, peeled and cubed
3 cups half and half
1 cup chicken stock
4 green onions, chopped

¼ cup fresh dill
Juice of 1 lemon
Zest of lemon

- ◆ Place all ingredients in a food processor until smooth.
- ◆ Chill overnight.
- ◆ Serve in soup bowls and garnish with fresh dill or chives.
- ◆ ½ teaspoon of curry can be added for additional flavor.

# Curried Chicken Soup

Serves 4-6

½ cup onion, chopped
½ cup celery, diced
½ cup carrots, diced
½ green pepper, chopped
2 apples, peeled, cored and diced
2 Tbls. butter
1 Tbls. flour
1 Tbls. curry powder

1 quart chicken stock
2 large tomatoes, diced
2 whole cloves
1 teaspoon salt
1 Tbls. fresh parsley
¼ teaspoon pepper
2 cups cooked chicken, diced
1 cup cream

- In a large pot melt the butter. Add the onion, celery, carrots, green pepper, and apples. Cook until tender.
- Add flour and curry powder. Add chicken stock, tomatoes, cloves, parsley, salt and pepper. Remove from heat. Cool.
- Pour into a food processor and blend until smooth.
- Place in soup tureen and stir in chicken and cream. Garnish with parsley.
- This can be served chilled or hot.

# Cream of Asparagus Soup

Serve 4

1 cucumber, peeled and cubed
4 green onions, chopped
½ pound asparagus
½ teaspoon salt

¼ teaspoon fresh ground pepper
2 Tbls. fresh dill
2 cups heavy cream
2 cups chicken stock

- Place all the ingredients in a food processor until smooth. Chill.
- Serve in soup bowls garnished with fresh dill.

# Seafood

**Lobster Boat – Straight Wharf**

Nantucket has an abundance of seafood, though much of the fishing has moved further offshore due to depleted supplies. However, on island one can still find mussels, crab, scallops and clams. As a child we would wander down to the Jetties to find mussels for dinner. Sadly the Jetties are now off-limit for climbing, prowling and even fishing. Permits are needed for mussels, scallops, clams, and oysters. Mussels and quahaugs have an open season; scallops, a commercial season November 1- to March 31; and oysters, September 1 to April 30.

The bay scallop is one of Nantucket's favorite delights. These succulently small shellfish have been around the island for many years, but were not shipped off island until the 1880s. Scalloping as an island profession really got started in 1881. The sea scallop found from Newfoundland to North Carolina is named the *Placopecten magellanicus*.

Codfish has long been a staple for the island. In earlier times cod was salted and dried to last for a longer period of time. Much of the cod from the Massachusetts Bay Colony was shipped to Portugal. Today codfish cakes are still an island favorite.

Even though lobsters were caught in abundance off the coast of Massachusetts they were once thought of as poor people's food. Today you almost have to rob a bank to finance a lobster dinner.

Whales were caught not only for food, but later sperm whales became known for their oil and Nantucket rose in importance as a whaling port. Whalebone became much sought after following the Civil War and could fetch alarmingly high prices. The Whaling Museum highlights the history of whaling.

Unique to Nantucket are the graceful catboats that were first built in New York. The single-masted boats were used for fishing, lobstering, scalloping, and today as part of the Rainbow fleet. They have a shallow draft which allows them to maneuver in Nantucket's shallow waters. *Lilian*, a 40 foot catboat, once carried passengers between Straight Wharf and Wauwinet. An early Herreshoff catboat dating from 1860 still survives, though not on island. Many of the island boats were built by the Crosby family in Osterville c 1835-1935. The Beetle cats were built by John Beetle from the 1920s-40s. The Rainbows are now built by the Concordia Yacht Yard in New Bedford. Today, instead of fishing, they can be seen racing on week-ends, and a number are now made of fiberglass instead of wood.

**Labor Day Dinner**

*Mussels*
*Bluefish Pate*
*Grilled Swordfish*
*Roasted Potatoes*
*Green Salad*
*Blueberry Peach Brown Betty*

# Grilled Swordfish

Serves 6

2½ pounds swordfish
1 cup mayonnaise

¼ cup lemon juice
¼ cup fresh dill

- Combine mayonnaise, lemon juice and dill in a bowl. Spread on both sides of the swordfish.
- Grill swordfish until cooked through.
- Place on a fish platter. Garnish with fresh dill sprigs.

# Grilled Swordfish with Salsa

Grill swordfish as explained in recipe above.

*Salsa*

4 large tomatoes, diced
1 avocado, peeled, stoned, and diced
½ cup red onion, chopped
Salt and pepper, to taste

2 green chilies, seeded and chopped
2 Tbls. cilantro
2 Tbls. olive oil
2 Tbls. lime juice

- Combine the ingredients in a bowl, or food processor until still chunky.
- Serve with the swordfish.

# Swordfish with Basil Butter

Serves 4

2 pounds swordfish
¼ cup mayonnaise

Juice of 1 lemon
8 ounces sun dried tomatoes

- ♦ Combine the lemon juice and mayonnaise and brush on each side of the swordfish.
- ♦ Grill the swordfish. Place on a fish platter for serving.

*Basil Butter*

¼ cup dry white wine
½ stick butter, softened

¼ cup fresh basil, chopped

- ♦ Combine the ingredients in a bowl.
- ♦ As soon as the swordfish comes off the grill brush the basil butter on fish. Top with sundried tomatoes.

# Skewered Swordfish

Serves 4

1 onion, chopped finely
Juice of 1 lemon
¼ cup olive oil
1 teaspoon salt

½ teaspoon pepper
2 pounds swordfish, cut into 1 inch cubes

- ♦ In a bowl combine the onions, lemon juice, olive oil, salt and pepper.
- ♦ Add the fish and marinate for 2 hours refrigerated.
- ♦ Slide the fish cubes onto skewers and grill.
- ♦ Serve with salsa, tartar sauce, or butter sauce for fish.
- ♦ The fish also can be grilled with vegetables or alternating with shrimp or scallops.

# Swordfish with Island Sauce

Serves 4-6

2 pounds swordfish
1 Tbls. butter
1 Tbls. flour
1 cup milk
½ teaspoon salt
½ teaspoon pepper

1 Tbls. curry
1 ounce crystallized ginger, cut into small pieces
2 small bananas, sliced
Juice of ½ lemon

- Grill the swordfish on a grill. Place on a serving platter.
- In a saucepan melt the butter and add the flour, stirring until smooth. Gradually stir in the milk. Add the other ingredients.
- Pour the sauce over the fish, and serve immediately.
- Any type of firm fish can be substituted for the swordfish.

# Swordfish with Chive Butter Sauce

Serves 4

2 pounds swordfish
Juice of 1 lemon

½ cup mayonnaise

- Combine the lemon juice and mayonnaise.
- Brush on swordfish.
- Grill swordfish

*Chive Butter*

¼ cup white wine vinegar
¼ cup dry white wine
2 Tbls. heavy cream
1 Tbls. shallot, chopped

½ stick butter
1 Tbls. lemon juice
Salt and pepper
2 Tbls. chives, minced

- In a skillet reduce the vinegar and wine. Add the shallots.
- Whisk in the cream, and then butter.
- Add the other ingredients until thickened.
- Brush on top side of swordfish as soon as it comes off the grill.
- Garnish with lemon slices and fresh chopped chives.

# Swordfish with Spinach Sauce

Serves 4

2 pounds swordfish                    ½ cup mayonnaise
Juice of 1 lemon

- Combine the lemon juice and mayonnaise.
- Brush on swordfish.
- Grill swordfish

*Spinach Sauce*

2 Tbls. olive oil                     1 cup chicken stock
2 Tbls. butter                        ½ pound fresh spinach, finely
2 Tbls. onion, finely chopped         chopped, no stems
2 cloves garlic, minced               ¼ cup fresh basil, finely
¼ cup dry white wine                  chopped
1 cup heavy cream

- In a skillet heat the olive oil and butter. Add the onion and garlic and saute until translucent.
- Stir in white wine and reduce to one-half.
- Add stock and cream. Stir until slightly thickened.
- Stir in spinach and basil.
- Serve in a bowl with the swordfish, or spread over swordfish just before serving.

# Mussels in Wine Sauce

Serves 4

4 pounds mussels in shell
2 Tbls. olive oil
2 Tbls. butter
2 shallots, finely chopped

2 cloves garlic, finely chopped
¾ cup dry white wine
¼ cup fresh parsley
Salt and pepper

- Make sure all the mussels are closed. Wash and pull off any beards on the mussels.
- Heat the olive oil and butter in a large pan and saute the shallots and garlic.
- Pour in the wine and add mussels. Bring to a boil. Add the parsley. Cook for 5 minutes or until mussels are opened. Season with salt and pepper.
- Serve with crusty French or Portuguese bread.
- The mussels can also be served over linguine.

# Mussels and Rice

Serves 6

1 cup olive oil
2 cups onions, chopped
1 cup pine nuts
3 cups cooked rice
1 cup dried cranberries

½ teaspoon cinnamon
¼ teaspoon allspice
1 teaspoon salt
6 dozen mussels in shells
1 cup dry white wine

- In a large skillet heat the olive oil and cook onions until translucent.
- Stir in the rest of the ingredients, except mussels.
- Rinse and scrub the mussels.
- In a large pot bring the mussels and wine to a boil. Continue cooking until the mussels open their shells. Remove from heat. At this point the shells can be discarded, or left on.
- Add the mussels and liquid to the rice mixture. Serve hot or chilled.

# Mussels and Cod

Serves 4-6

2 Tbls. olive oil
2 Tbls. butter
1 onion, chopped
3 cloves garlic, crushed
¼ cup flour
½ teaspoon paprika

2 pounds cod, cut into bitesize pieces
2 cups fish stock
½ cup dry white wine
3 pounds mussels
¼ cup fresh parsley, chopped
Salt and pepper

- ◆ Wash and clean the mussels.
- ◆ In a skillet heat the oil and butter. Add the onion and cook until tender. Add garlic.
- ◆ On a plate combine the flour and paprika. Dip the cod in the mixture. Add to the onion and garlic in the frying pan. Fry until golden.
- ◆ Stir in the stock, wine, salt and pepper.
- ◆ Add the mussels and parsley. Cook until the mussels open.
- ◆ Serve in bowls with Portuguese bread to soak up the liquid.

# Mussels Marinara

Serves 4

4 pounds mussels in shell
1 cup dry white wine
1 carrot, thinly sliced
1 onion, chopped
¼ cup olive oil
4 cloves garlic, minced

4 large ripe tomatoes, finely chopped
¼ cup fresh basil, chopped
1 teaspoon oregano
Salt and pepper

- ◆ Wash mussels and remove beards.
- ◆ Heat the wine in a large pot and add mussels. Bring to a boil and cook 5 minutes, or until mussels are opened.
- ◆ In a large pot heat the olive oil and add the carrot and onion.
- ◆ Add the garlic and tomatoes, until tomatoes are softened.
- ◆ Add the basil, oregano, salt and pepper. Add mussels.
- ◆ Serve warm over linguini or with French bread.

# Nantucket Clambake

Nantucket clambakes are a traditional pastime of the summer. Though not as frequent as they used to be every Nantucket family has memories of how they sat around the fire, and awaited the moment when the seaweed was removed and the eating could begin.

The basic ingredients for a clambake are lobster, clams, corn on the cob, and potatoes. Add to this a salad, Portuguese bread, butter, salt and pepper, followed by watermelon and fruit. One can never feel underfed. Start early in the afternoon on preparation.

*The Clambake*

Serves 12

24 ears of corn
12 1½ pound lobsters
12 large baking potatoes

6 dozen clams in shell
Melted butter
Lemons

- ♦ On Nantucket you do need a permit for a fire, so make sure this is in hand, before finding the perfect beach site for your gathering.
- ♦ Dig a large hole in the sand and line with any rocks you can find on the beach.
- ♦ Add driftwood and hardwood charcoal. Start a fire.
- ♦ Walk along the beach and gather seaweed.
- ♦ After an hour or two the rocks will get quite hot. Cover them with some of the seaweed. Place the lobsters on top. Cover with more seaweed. Add the clams. Add more seaweed, then foil covered potatoes and corn in their husks.
- ♦ Cover with a tarpaulin weighted down with stones. Bake for 1 hour. Make sure the clams have opened their shells.
- ♦ Serve immediately.

# Scallops Almondine

Serves 4

2 pounds bay scallops
¼ cup onion, minced
2 Tbls. butter
1 cup heavy cream
¼ cup dry sherry

¼ cup parsley
½ cup slivered almonds
¼ cup freshly grated parmesan cheese
2-3 cups cooked rice

- Preheat broiler.
- In a skillet melt the butter and add onion, stirring until translucent.
- Stir in cream and sherry. Add scallops. Place in a casserole. Sprinkle with almonds and cheese.
- Put under broiler to just brown.
- Remove and garnish with parsley. Serve immediately with rice.

# Skewered Scallops

Serves 4-6

2 pounds sea scallops
¼ cup lemon juice
¼ cup dry Vermouth
1 clove garlic, minced
2 Tbls. fresh parsley
½ lb. small mushroom caps

1 pint cherry tomatoes
1 green pepper, cut up
1 red bell pepper, cut up
1 large onion, cubed
Skewers

- In a bowl combine the lemon juice, Vermouth, garlic and parsley. Coat the scallops with the mixture.
- On skewers alternate the scallops with the vegetables.
- Grill.
- Serve with rice

# Bay Scallops in Puff Pastry

Serves 6

2 pounds Bay scallops
1 pound fresh spinach
2 tomatoes, chopped finely
2 cloves garlic, minced
Juice of 1 lemon

2 Tbls. olive oil
2 Tbls. butter
Puff pastry
1 egg, beaten

- Preheat the oven to 425°.
- In a skillet heat the olive oil and butter. Quickly saute the tomatoes, spinach and garlic. Stir in the scallops and lemon juice.
- Roll out the pastry into six squares, each about ¼" thick.
- Spread the scallop mixture in the center of the pastry.
- Dampen the edges of the pastry, fold over scallops and press to seal edges.
- Place on a baking sheet and brush with the egg.
- Bake in the oven for 25 minutes or until pastry is browned.

*Lobster Cream Sauce*

1 pound lobster meat
1 cup heavy cream
¼ cup flour

½ stick butter
½ cup Sherry

- Melt the butter in a sauce pan.
- Add the flour and stir in the cream and Sherry until thickened.
- Fold in the lobster.
- Serve with the scallops in puff pastry.

# Coquilles

Serves 4

1 pound bay scallops
½ pound mushrooms, sliced
1 Tbls. shallot, chopped
1 cup dry white wine
1 stick butter

2 cups cream
½ cup flour
Salt and pepper to taste
¼ teaspoon cayenne

- ◆ Preheat broiler.
- ◆ In a skillet melt 2 Tbls. butter. Add the mushrooms and saute for 3 minutes.
- ◆ Add the scallops, shallots and wine, and cook for 5 minutes.
- ◆ Add the cream and bring to a boil. Season with salt, pepper, and cayenne.
- ◆ In a saucepan melt the remaining butter and stir in flour. Pour this into the scallop mixture and cook for 2 minutes. When this has thickened pour the mixture into 6 large scallop shells.
- ◆ Place under broiler until just browned.
- ◆ Serve on fish plates and garnish with parsley.

# Scallop Ceviche

Serves 4 or more

2 pounds Bay scallops
1 cup fresh lime juice
¼ cup olive oil
¼ cup scallion, finely chopped
¼ cup parsley, finely chopped
2 cloves garlic, crushed

1 green chili, seeded and chopped
½ teaspoon salt
Dash of Tabasco sauce
2 Tbls. cilantro, chopped
1 avocado, peeled, pitted and finely chopped

- ◆ In a bowl combine all the ingredients.
- ◆ Refrigerate for at least 4 hours.
- ◆ Serve with a salad and hot rolls.
- ◆ The ceviche also can be served as an appetizer.

# Scallops in Wine Sauce

Serves 4-6

2 pounds scallops
2 shallots, chopped
½ cup chervil, chopped
½ stick butter
¼ cup flour

Salt and pepper
½ cup dry white wine
1 cup heavy cream
3 cups cooked rice

♦ In a sauce pan heat the wine and add the scallops. Bring to a boil. Remove from heat.
♦ In another sauce pan melt the butter and saute the shallots.
♦ Stir in the flour and add cream until thickened.
♦ Add scallops, wine, chervil and salt and pepper.
♦ Serve hot over rice.


# Scallop Casserole

Serves 4

1 stick butter
½ cup flour
2 cups cream
½ cup sharp cheddar cheese, grated
½ teaspoon salt

Pepper, to taste
¼ teaspoon dry mustard
2 Tbls. Worcestershire sauce
¼ cup sherry
2 pounds scallops
¼ cup fresh bread crumbs

♦ Preheat oven to 350°.
♦ In a saucepan melt the butter. Stir in flour and then cream. Add cheddar cheese and stir until melted. Add salt, pepper, mustard, Worcestershire sauce and sherry.
♦ Place the scallops in a casserole.
♦ Pour the sauce over the scallops. Top with bread crumbs.
♦ Bake for ½ hour or until just browned and bubbly.
♦ Serve with rice.

# Broiled Lobster

Serves 4

4 uncooked lobster tails                    ¼ cup unsalted butter, melted

- Preheat the broiler.
- Place the lobster tails, meat side up, with the melted butter. Turn over lobster tails.
- Broil for 5 minutes. Turn and broil other side for another 5 minutes. Remove from oven.
- Place on a fish platter and garnish with lemon slices.

# Lobster with Herbed Mayonnaise

Serves 4

4 lobsters

- Cook lobsters in boiling water for 12-15 minutes.
- Remove and place on separate plates, or fish platter. Serve with herbed mayonnaise and lemon slices.

*Herbed Mayonnaise*

1 clove garlic                    1 teaspoon dry mustard
¼ cup fresh dill                  2 Tbls. vinegar
Juice of ½ lemon                  1 cup mayonnaise
2 Tbls. chives

- In food processor combine the ingredients until smooth.
- Serve in a bowl with the lobster.

# Lobster Thermidor

Serves 4

4 lobsters
2 Tbls. butter

½ cup bread crumbs
Parmesan cheese

- Fill a large pot with 2 inches water. Bring the water to a boil and add lobsters.
- Cook 12-15 minutes. Remove from heat.
- Carefully split the lobsters in half and remove the meat.
- In a sauce pan melt the butter and saute the lobster meat for 2 minutes. Add the bechamel sauce.
- Stuff the lobster shells with the lobster mixture. Cover with bread crumbs, a dot of butter and freshly grated parmesan cheese.
- Bake in 350° oven for 15 minutes, or under broiler until just browned.
- Serve on individual plates with rice or freshly baked bread.

*Bechamel Sauce*

1 cup fish stock
1 carrot, sliced
1 onion, sliced
2 bay leaves
¼ cup fresh parsley
6 peppercorns
½ stick butter
½ cup flour

1 cup cream
½ teaspoon salt
½ teaspoon pepper
1 Tbls. Dijon mustard
2 Tbls. scallion, chopped
¾ cup Sherry
¼ cup Cognac
2 egg yolks

- In a sauce pan cook the stock, onion, carrot, bay leaves, parsley and peppercorns for 20 minutes. Remove from heat and strain.
- Melt the butter and slowly stir in the flour. Add stock, cream, mustard, scallion, Sherry, Cognac, egg yolks, and salt and pepper to taste.

# Steamed Lobster

Have available lobster crackers, picks, bibs and bowls for the lobster shells

At the end of the meal provide everyone with a finger bowl – a bowl with warm water and lemon juice, and a finger towel.

- You will need a large pot
- Fill with 2" water
- Bring water to a boil
- Drop in lobsters, one at a time.
- Cover pot
- Cook for 12-15 minutes, until the lobsters have turned bright red
- Remove immediately
- Let cool or serve hot
- Serve with melted butter or lemon wedges

# Stuffed Flounder

3 pounds flounder fillets
2 dozen quahaugs
1 stick butter, melted
1 cup celery, chopped
1 cup onion, chopped
1 cup bread crumbs

½ cup green pepper, chopped
½ cup red pepper
¼ cup parsley, chopped
½ teaspoon fresh thyme
Salt and pepper

- Line a greased casserole with the flounder.
- Place the quahaugs on a cookie sheet and place in oven until shells open. Remove clams from shells and chop clams finely.
- In a bowl combine the quahaugs, butter, celery, onion, green pepper, red pepper, parsley, thyme, and salt and pepper to taste.
- Spread over the fish fillets.
- Bake for 30 minutes.
- Serve on a fish platter. Garnish with parsley sprigs.

**Summer Night Dinner**

*Clam Chowder*
*Baked Bluefish*
*Roasted Potatoes*
*Corn on the Cob*
*Mixed Greens Salad*
*Portuguese Bread*
*Blueberry Pie*

# Baked Bluefish

Serves 6-8

3 pounds bluefish fillets
1 teaspoon salt
1 large onion, chopped
1 green pepper, chopped
¼ cup parsley, chopped
2 cloves garlic, chopped
1 cup fine bread crumbs

2 large tomatoes, finely chopped
½ teaspoon pepper
½ cup walnuts
Juice of 1 lemon
¼ cup olive oil
1 lemon, sliced

- ◆ Preheat oven to 350°.
- ◆ Place the bluefish in a baking dish. Rub with the salt.
- ◆ In a bowl combine all the other ingredients except lemon slices. Spoon the mixture over the fish.
- ◆ Bake for 35-40 minutes, until fish is just browned. Do not overcook.
- ◆ Remove and place on fish platter. Garnish with lemon slices.

# Seafood Casserole

6 Servings

| | |
|---|---|
| 1 stick butter | 3 Tbls. flour |
| 3 shallots, chopped | 1 Tbls. curry powder |
| 1 green pepper, chopped | 1 cup cream |
| ¼ pound mushrooms, sliced | 1 pound scallops |
| 4 pounds flounder fillets | 2 tomatoes, sliced |
| Salt and pepper to taste | ¼ cup freshly grated parmesan |
| ¼ cup dry white wine | cheese |

- Preheat the oven to 350°.
- Melt ½ stick butter in a skillet and saute mushrooms, shallots and green pepper. Add the fish filets. Pour the wine over the fish and simmer for 10 minutes.
- In a saucepan melt the remaining butter and stir in the flour and curry powder. Add the cream. Cook until thickened.
- Transfer the fish and vegetables to a casserole. Add the liquid to the cream mixture.
- Place the scallops on the fish and pour the sauce over the scallops. Top with the tomatoes and parmesan cheese.
- Bake ½ hour or until just browned.
- Serve with rice.

# Salmon with Horseradish Sauce

Serves 6

| | |
|---|---|
| 3 pounds salmon fillets | ¼ cup olive oil |
| ½ cup red wine vinegar | ¼ cup heavy cream |
| 1 Tbls. sugar | 2 Tbls. horseradish |
| 2 Tbls. capers | 1 Tbls. fresh dill |
| ¼ cup lemon juice | Salt and pepper, to taste |

- Combine all the ingredients except for the salmon in a bowl. Cover and refrigerate.
- Broil, grill or smoke the salmon.
- Serve on a fish platter with the horseradish sauce in a separate bowl.

# Salmon with Spinach and Salsa

Serves 4

4 6 oz. salmon fillets               2 Tbls. lemon juice
2 Tbls. olive oil

- ◆ Brush the salmon with the olive oil and lemon juice.
- ◆ Either grill or broil the fish.
- ◆ On individual plates divide up the spinach.
- ◆ Place the salmon on top. Cover with salsa.
- ◆ Serve immediately.

1 pound fresh spinach               2 Tbls. olive oil

In a skillet saute the spinach in the olive oil.

*Salsa*

½ cup fresh basil                    2 green chilies, seeded and
2 cloves garlic, crushed             chopped
2 large tomatoes, chopped            2 scallions, chopped
2 Tbls. olive oil                    Salt and pepper
                                     ¼ cup cilantro, chopped

- ◆ Combine ingredients in a bowl.

# Salmon on a Bed of Spinach with Hollandaise Sauce

Serves 8

4 pounds salmon fillets
2 pounds fresh spinach, without stems

Sesame oil
Hollandaise Sauce (p.202)

- Grill or smoke the salmon fillets.
- In a wok pour a small amount of sesame oil. Heat wok. Slowly stir fry the spinach, small batches at a time.
- Place the spinach on a fish platter.
- Lay the salmon on top of the spinach. Pour the Hollandaise sauce over the salmon.
- This can be served hot or cold.

# Cod with Mint Salsa

Serves 4

2 pounds fresh cod
Juice of 1 lemon

¼ cup mayonnaise

- Combine the lemon juice and mayonnaise and brush over cod.
- Grill the cod.

*Mint Salsa*

1 bunch basil leaves
8 mint leaves
2 cloves garlic

¼ cup olive oil
Salt and pepper
Juice of 1 lime

- In a food processor combine the ingredients until smooth.
- Serve with the cod.

# Tuna with Pineapple Salsa

Serves 4

2 pounds tuna
Juice of 1 lime

¼ cup mayonnaise

- ♦ Combine the mayonnaise and lime juice.
- ♦ Brush over tuna.
- ♦ Grill the tuna.

*Pineapple Salsa*

2 cups fresh pineapple, finely chopped
2 green chilies, seeded and chopped finely

2 Tbls fresh cilantro, chopped
Juice of 1 lime
2 Tbls. green onion, chopped
2 cloves garlic, minced

- ♦ In a bowl combine all the ingredients.
- ♦ Serve with the tuna.
- ♦ Swordfish or any fish can be substituted for the tuna.

# Tuna with Mango Lime Butter

Serves 4

2 pounds tuna

Juice of 1 lime

- ♦ Broil or grill the tuna, brushed with lime juice.

*Mango Lime Butter*

1 stick unsalted butter, softened
1 mango, peeled, cored and finely chopped

Juice of 1 lime

- ♦ In a bowl combine the ingredients.
- ♦ Spoon over the tuna after it has been cooked, and serve immediately.

# Tuna with Mushrooms

Serves 4

½ stick butter
2 pounds tuna
2 cloves garlic, minced
½ pound mushrooms, sliced
1 teaspoon thyme

2 Tbls. fresh parsley
2 Tbls. fresh chives, snipped
1 teaspoon tarragon

- ♦ Preheat oven to 350°.
- ♦ In a skillet melt the butter and saute the mushrooms and garlic. Add the parsley, thyme, chives and tarragon.
- ♦ Place the fish in a baking dish and cover with mushroom mixture.
- ♦ Bake for 25 minutes, or until desired doneness.
- ♦ Serve with rice.

# Jambalaya

Serves 8

¼ pound bacon
2 large onions, chopped
1 green pepper, chopped
1 red bell pepper, chopped
2 cups uncooked rice
1 16 ounce can tomatoes
2 cups chicken stock
4 cloves, garlic, minced
1 teaspoon salt

1 teaspoon fresh ground pepper
½ teaspoon cayenne
½ cup bourbon
1 pound fresh mussels
1 pound scallops
1 pound medium shrimp, peeled and deveined
1 pound salmon, cut into bite size pieces

- ♦ Preheat oven to 350°.
- ♦ In a dutch oven saute bacon until just browned. Remove bacon and break into small pieces. Add onions to pan and saute in bacon fat until translucent.
- ♦ Add peppers and cook for 4 minutes. Add rice, tomatoes, chicken stock, bourbon, garlic, salt and pepper. Gently stir in seafood.
- ♦ Bake for 40 minutes or until rice is tender. More chicken stock may need to be added. Serve immediately.

# Garlicy Shrimp

Serves 6

2½ pounds jumbo shrimp
1 cup dry white wine
2 tomatoes, finely chopped
4 garlic cloves, crushed
2 shallots, chopped finely

½ pound mushrooms, sliced
¼ cup olive oil
¼ cup fresh basil, chopped
Juice of 1 lemon
4 cups cooked rice

- ◆ In a skillet saute the mushrooms, garlic and shallots in the olive oil.
- ◆ Add the shrimp and cook for 4 minutes.
- ◆ Add the wine, basil and lemon juice.
- ◆ Serve over rice in a serving bowl, or on individual plates.

# Fried Oysters with Dill Tartar Sauce

Serves 4

1 quart oysters
1 teaspoon onion powder
2 Tbls. milk
2 eggs
1 cup fine cracker crumbs

2 Tbls. fresh parsley, chopped
Salt and pepper
Oil for frying
Lemon wedges

- ◆ Drain the oysters.
- ◆ Combine the eggs, milk and onion powder in a bowl.
- ◆ In another bowl combine the cracker crumbs and parsley.
- ◆ Dip the oysters in the egg mixture, then the cracker crumbs.
- ◆ Heat the oil to 375°. Fry the oysters until golden brown.
- ◆ Serve with lemon wedges and tartar sauce.

*Tartar Sauce*

1 cup mayonnaise
¼ cup fresh dill, snipped
2 Tbls. fresh lemon juice

2 Tbls. pickle relish
2 Tbls. capers

- ◆ Combine the ingredients in a bowl. Serve with oysters or other seafood.

# Fowl

**The Hadwen House – 96 Main Street, once owned by the author's family and now part of the Nantucket Historical Association**

# Grilled Chicken Breasts with Vegetables

Serves 6

6 boneless chicken breasts
1 cup onion, chopped
½ pound mushrooms, sliced
2 large tomatoes, sliced
4 cloves garlic, minced
1 green pepper, sliced

1 red bell pepper, sliced
½ cup fresh basil, chopped
½ stick butter
½ pound Mozzarella cheese, shredded

- ♦ Grill the chicken breasts.
- ♦ In a large skillet melt the butter and saute the vegetables.
- ♦ Place the chicken breasts in a casserole.
- ♦ Top with vegetables and then cheese.
- ♦ Place under broiler until just browned.
- ♦ Or bake in 350° oven until browned.

# Chicken Florentine

Serves 6

6 boneless chicken breasts
½ pound mushrooms, sliced
1 pound fresh spinach, blanched
½ stick butter
½ cup flour

1 cup heavy cream
1 cup chicken stock
¼ cup Sherry
½ teaspoon nutmeg

- ♦ Preheat oven to 350°
- ♦ In a sauce pan melt the butter and stir in the flour.
- ♦ Slowly add the stock and cream until thickened.
- ♦ Add Sherry and nutmeg.
- ♦ In a buttered casserole combine the mushrooms and spinach.
- ♦ Top with the chicken breasts. Pour the sauce over the chicken.
- ♦ Bake for 45 minutes.
- ♦ Serve with pasta or rice.

# Chicken Pie

Serves 4-6

| | |
|---|---|
| 4 cups cooked chicken, diced | ½ cup celery, thinly sliced |
| ½ cup green pepper, chopped | 2 Tbls. dill |
| 1 onion, chopped | 2 cups chicken broth |
| 2 cloves garlic, chopped | ½ cup flour |
| ½ cup red bell pepper, chopped | ½ stick butter |
| ½ cup carrots, thinly sliced | Salt and pepper |

- Preheat oven to 350°.
- In a skillet melt the butter and saute the onion, peppers, carrots, celery, and garlic until just tender.
- Add the flour and slowly stir in the chicken broth until thickened.
- Stir in the chicken, dill, salt and pepper to season.
- Spoon into a casserole. Top with crust.
- Bake for 45 minutes or until crust is just browned.

*Crust*

| | |
|---|---|
| 1 cup flour | ½ cup sharp cheddar cheese, grated |
| 2 teaspoons baking powder | ¼ cup fresh dill |
| ¼ cup half and half | 3 Tbls. butter |

- Put all the ingredients in a food processor. Blend until a ball is formed. More milk can be added if ball does not form.
- Roll out on a cutting board in the shape of casserole you will be using and place in casserole.

# Coq au Vin

Serves 6-8

| | |
|---|---|
| 1 4-pound chicken | ¼ teaspoon cinnamon |
| 1 stick butter | ¼ teaspoon cloves |
| 2 apples, peeled, cored and cubed | ¼ teaspoon nutmeg |
| | ¼ teaspoon dried sage |
| 4 slices bacon | 1 cup Calvados |
| 1 dozen small white onions | 1 cup chicken broth |
| 1 clove garlic, mashed | Salt and pepper to taste |

- ◆ Cut chicken into 8 pieces.
- ◆ Cook bacon and add onions until translucent in a large skillet.
- ◆ Remove bacon and onion. Break bacon into small pieces.
- ◆ Add chicken and butter to skillet. Brown chicken. Add bacon, onion, garlic, Calvados, chicken broth and apples.
- ◆ Season with salt, pepper and spices.
- ◆ Simmer for about 1 hour.

# Cranberry Chicken Livers

My oldest friend, Quinnie Hallett and I love to share recipes. I think this was the first one we exchanged back in 1968.

4 servings

| | |
|---|---|
| 1 pound ground beef | ½ teaspoon garlic powder |
| 1 pound chicken livers | Salt and pepper |
| 1 cup cranberry jelly | ½ teaspoon oregano |
| 1 8-ounce can tomato sauce | 1 8-ounce package egg noodles |
| ½ teaspoon onion powder | |

- ◆ Cook the beef in a skillet and then add chicken livers until browned.
- ◆ Melt the cranberry jelly in a saucepan, and add tomato sauce and herbs and spices.
- ◆ Pour the sauce over the beef and livers.
- ◆ Garnish with parsley.
- ◆ Serve with noodles, cooked according to the directions on the package.

# Cranberry Chicken Mold

This is a lovely mold for a lady's luncheon.

Serves 6-8

2 cups cranberry orange sauce (p. 192)
4 cups cooked chicken, chopped
¼ cup onions, chopped
1 cup slivered almonds
4 packages unflavored gelatin

½ cup water
1 cup celery, diced
¾ cup mayonnaise
3 cans cream of chicken soup
Salt and pepper, to taste

♦ In a bowl mash the cranberry orange sauce with a fork.
♦ In a bowl combine 2 of the packages of gelatin that have been softened in water.
♦ Add cranberry orange sauce.
♦ Pour into a large mold. Cool in refrigerator until firm.
♦ In a bowl combine all the remaining ingredients. Pour over the cranberry mold. Chill until firm.
♦ Unmold onto a platter.
♦ Garnish with parsley. Serve with mayonnaise.


# Grilled Chicken Breasts

Serves 6

6 boneless chicken breasts
½ pound Prosciutto ham

1 pound sundried tomatoes
1 cup heavy cream

♦ Grill the chicken breasts. Place on a platter. Top with slices of prosciutto.
♦ In a food processor combine the tomatoes and cream. Pour over the prosciutto.
♦ Serve immediately or chilled.

# Stir-Fry Chicken

Serves 6

2½ pounds boneless chicken breasts, cut into bitesize pieces
2 cups fresh corn
1 zucchini, sliced thinly
1 red bell pepper, sliced
1 green pepper, sliced
2 scallions, sliced

2 cloves garlic, minced
¼ cup soy sauce
¼ cup dry Sherry
1 Tbls. fresh ginger
Dash of cayenne
Sesame oil
Rice

♦ In a bowl combine the scallions, garlic, soy sauce, Sherry, ginger and cayenne.
♦ Add the chicken and allow to marinate refrigerated for at least 2 hours.
♦ Heat a wok with a small amount of sesame oil. Quickly stir-fry the chicken until cooked through. Remove and place in a bowl.
♦ Add more oil and stir-fry the vegetables. Add chicken to warm.
♦ Serve with rice.

# Poulet Almondine

Serves 4

4 chicken breasts
½ stick butter
¼ cup sherry
1 small can tomato paste
2 Tbls. flour

Salt and pepper
½ cup chicken stock
¾ cup sour cream
¾ cup sliced almonds
1 bay leaf

♦ Preheat oven to 350°.
♦ In a skillet melt the butter. Add chicken and brown. Add sherry. Remove chicken from skillet.
♦ To skillet add flour, salt, pepper and stock and bring to a boil.
♦ Add sour cream and ¼ cup almonds.
♦ Put chicken in a casserole.
♦ Top with sauce from skillet. Sprinkle with rest of almonds.
♦ Bake 20 minutes. Serve with rice or noodles.

# Cranberry Duck

Serves 4

1 duck (4 or more pounds)

- Preheat oven to 450°.
- Put the duck neck and giblets in a heavy sauce pan with 4 cups of water and simmer for at least two hours.
- Rub the duck with kosher salt and put in a roasting pan.
- Roast for 15 minutes and then reduce heat to 350° and cook for one hour and 15 minutes. Draw off the fat as it bakes.
- Remove the duck when done and reserve stock, removing some fat, in the roasting pan.
- Slice the duck.

*Cranberry Sauce*

1½ cups duck stock
Juice and zest of 1 lemon
1 cup cranberry chutney (p.192)

1 pear, peeled and chopped
½ cup bourbon

- When the duck is finished roasting, heat the duck stock with the duck drippings.
- Add the chutney, lemon juice and zest, pear and bourbon.
- Put the sliced duck back in the roasting pan and coat with the sauce.
- Bake for another 15 minutes.
- Place on a platter and garnish with parsley and fresh cranberries.
- Serve the extra sauce in a sauceboat.
- The sauce can also be served with chicken or goose.

**Christmas Dinner**

*Eggnog*
*Oysters on the Half Shell*
*Pate*
*Curried Squash Soup*
*Roast Goose with Orange Sauce*
*Cranberry Nut Salad*
*Crab Stuffed Potatoes*
*Sauteed Spinach*
*Apple Cranberry Pie*
*Ginger Mousse*
*Plum Pudding*

# Roast Goose with Orange Sauce

Serves 6

| | |
|---|---|
| 8 pound goose | 1 onion, sliced |
| 1 apple, cored and sliced | Coarse salt |

- Heat the oven to 350°.
- Rinse the goose. Rub the skin with the salt.
- Place the apples and onion in the cavity.
- Put the goose in a roasting pan and bake 20 minutes to pound, until crisp on outside.

*Orange Sauce*

| | |
|---|---|
| Grated rind of one orange | ½ cup sugar |
| 1 cup dry white wine | 1 Tbls. white wine vinegar |
| ½ teaspoon ginger | 1 cup fresh orange juice |
| ½ teaspoon ground allspice | ¼ cup Grand Marnier |
| ½ teaspoon ground nutmeg | ¼ cup currant jelly |
| 1 Tbls. brown sugar | 2 Tbls. corn starch |

- Combine the orange rind, wine, ginger, allspice, nutmeg and brown sugar in a sauce pan. Simmer for 20 minutes.
- Dissolve the cornstarch in ¼ cup orange juice. Add the remaining ingredients, except for cornstarch. Stir in cornstarch and orange juice until the sauce is thickened. Serve with the goose or other fowl.

## Thanksgiving Dinner

*Cranberry Brie*
*Roasted Oysters and Scallops*
*Roast Turkey*
*Garlic Mashed Potatoes*
*Green Beans*
*Cranberry Salad*
*Cranberry Chutney*
*Cranberry Orange Sauce*
*Pumpkin Cheesecake*
*Mincemeat Pie*

# Roast Turkey

Serves 10 or more

15 pound turkey

- Preheat the oven to 350°.
- Rinse the turkey with cold water and remove the giblets and neck.
- Place the giblets and neck in a pan of water, cover, and simmer for at least two hours.
- Rub the turkey with kosher salt and put in roasting pan. Stuff with dressing. Bake 20 minutes to the pound.

*Stuffing*

½ pound sausage
1 large onion, chopped
½ stick butter
2 stalks celery, chopped
1 loaf white bread, broken into
bitesize pieces
½ teaspoon thyme
1 teaspoon sage

2 Tbls. poultry seasoning
¼ cup fresh parsley, chopped
1 cup chopped pecans
2 cups cranberries
1 apple, peeled, cored, and
chopped

- In a large skillet brown the sausage. Remove sausage. Melt the butter and saute the onion and celery. Add the other ingredients.
- Stuff the turkey with the dressing before cooking turkey.

*Herb Bread Stuffing*

½ stick butter
1 large onion, chopped
2 stalks celery, chopped
1 apple, peeled, cored, and diced
½ teaspoon sage

1 teaspoon thyme
1 teaspoon rosemary
1 loaf Nantucket herb bread, cut into 1" cubes

- ◆ Heat the butter in a skillet and saute the onion, celery and apple until tender.
- ◆ Add the bread until just browned. Add herbs.
- ◆ 1 cup pecans or walnuts can be added for a crunchier stuffing.

*Gravy*

- ◆ Remove the turkey from the roasting pan and reserve the stock. Heat the stock and stir in ¼ cup flour to thicken.
- ◆ Stir in stock from giblets and neck.
- ◆ Cut the meat off the neck and cut giblets into fine pieces. Add to stock. Serve hot in a sauceboat.

# Meats

**Ham and Biscuits at Orange Street Party**

**Easter Dinner**

*Eggs with Caviar*
*Baby Spinach Fingers*
*Grilled Lamb*
*Asparagus Salad*
*Crab Stuffed Potatoes*
*Assorted Breads*
*Strawberries Romanoff*

# Grilled Lamb with Garlic Cream Sauce

Serves 8

4 pounds boneless lamb
¼ cup fresh ground pepper
¼ cup fresh rosemary

½ teaspoon cayenne
1 teaspoon garlic powder
1 Tbls. kosher salt

- ♦ Combine the spices in a bowl. Rub into lamb.
- ♦ Grill lamb to desired pinkness.

*Garlic Cream Sauce*

4 cloves garlic, minced
½ cup dry white wine

1 cup heavy cream

- ♦ In a sauce pan heat the wine with the garlic cloves. Simmer for 10 minutes. Add the cream.
- ♦ Serve warm with the lamb.

# Lamb with Raspberry Pistachio Sauce

Serves 8-10

4 pounds boneless leg of lamb
2 teaspoons kosher salt

¼ cup fresh ground pepper
1 teaspoon garlic powder

- ◆ Combine salt, pepper and garlic in a bowl. Rub into lamb.
- ◆ Grill lamb to desired pinkness.

*Pistachio Sauce*

2 cups fresh raspberries
2 Tbls. balsamic vinegar

2 cups shelled pistachios

- ◆ Place ingredients in a food processor until well blended.
- ◆ Serve in a bowl with the lamb.

# Lamb Patties

Serves 8

3 pounds ground lamb
½ cup green pepper, chopped
½ cup red pepper, chopped
2 cloves garlic, minced

2 green onions, chopped
¼ cup pine nuts
Dijon mustard

- ◆ In a bowl combine the lamb, peppers, garlic, onion and pine nuts.
- ◆ Shape into patties.
- ◆ Grill until desired doneness.
- ◆ Serve with Dijon mustard or mint sauce (see Minted Lamb Patties)

# Minted Lamb Patties

Serves 8

3 pounds ground lamb
¼ cup fresh mint
2 cloves garlic

1 teaspoon kosher salt
1 teaspoon fresh ground pepper

- ◆ In a bowl combine all the ingredients. Shape into patties.
- ◆ Grill until desired doneness.

*Mint Sauce*

1 cup sour cream
¼ cup fresh mint, chopped

¼ cup fresh lime juice

- ◆ Combine all the ingredients in a bowl.
- ◆ Serve with the lamb patties.

# Lamb with Port Sauce

Serves 8-10

4 pounds boneless leg of lamb
¼ cup fresh ground pepper

2 Tbls. kosher salt

- ◆ Coat the lamb with the salt and pepper.
- ◆ Grill until desired doneness.

*Port Sauce*

1 cup Port
¾ cup fresh orange juice
¼ cup fresh lemon juice

½ cup red currant jelly
2 Tbls. orange rind
2 Tbls. lemon rind

- ◆ Combine ingredients in a sauce pan. Bring to a boil. Simmer 5 minutes. Let thicken.
- ◆ Serve with lamb.

## Cranberry Festival Dinner

*Scallops Wrapped in Bacon*
*Hot Brie*
*Grilled Pork Loin*
*Squash*
*Country Salad*
*Herb Bread*
*Cranberry Pie*

# Grilled Pork Tenderloin with Beach Plum Sauce

Serves 8

4 pounds pork tenderloin
¼ cup brown sugar
¼ cup fresh ground pepper

¼ teaspoon cayenne
2 Tbls. coarse salt

- ♦ In a bowl combine the sugar, pepper, cayenne and salt. Rub into the pork.
- ♦ Grill or roast the pork until desired doneness.

*Beach Plum Sauce*

1 jar beach plum jelly
Grated rind and juice of 1 lemon
Grated rind and juice of 1 orange

¼ cup port
2 Tbls. brandy
¼ teaspoon ginger
Salt and pepper

- ♦ Simmer the orange and lemon rinds and juices for 5 minutes in a saucepan.
- ♦ Add the jelly and stir until melted.
- ♦ Add the port and brandy.
- ♦ Season with the ginger, salt and pepper.
- ♦ Serve in a bowl with the pork.

# Cranberry Pork Chops

Serves 4

4 thick cut pork chops
½ cup bread crumbs

1 tablespoon rosemary
1 cup cranberry chutney

- ◆ Cut a pocket in the pork chops.
- ◆ Combine the chutney and bread crumbs.
- ◆ Stuff the pork chop pockets with the bread mixture. Sprinkle the pork chops with rosemary.
- ◆ Bake at 350° for 45 minutes.
- ◆ Serve on a platter with extra chutney.

# Pork Tenderloin with Cranberry Mustard

Serves 8

4 pounds pork tenderloin
2 teaspoons thyme
2 Tbls. garlic salt

2 Tbls. kosher salt
2 teaspoons ground ginger
2 Tbls. fresh ground pepper

- ◆ In a bowl combine the thyme, garlic salt, kosher salt, ginger and pepper. Rub into the pork.
- ◆ Grill or roast pork until desired pinkness.

*Cranberry Mustard*

1 cup Dijon mustard
1 cup cranberries, crushed

¼ cup white wine vinegar
¼ cup brown sugar

- ◆ In a sauce pan combine all the ingredients until the cranberries pop and sauce is thickened.
- ◆ Serve in a bowl with the pork.

# Pork Picatta

Serves 6

2 ½ pounds thinly sliced pork          ½ stick butter

- ◆ Melt the butter and quickly saute the pork. Remove from the pan.

*Sauce*

2 Tbls. olive oil                          2 medium tomatoes, chopped
1 small onion, chopped                1 Tbls. fresh parsley, chopped
1 clove garlic, chopped                1 Tbls. fresh basil, chopped
½ pound mushrooms                   Salt and pepper
1 14 ounce can artichoke hearts

- ◆ Heat the oil in a skillet and cook the onion until translucent.
- ◆ Add the other ingredients.
- ◆ Cook for 30 minutes or until the sauce is thickened. Serve over the pork.

# Roast Pork Tenderloin with Cider

Serves 6-8

3 pounds pork tenderloin              ¼ cup fresh ground pepper
2 cloves garlic, minced                 ½ cup apple cider
¼ cup fresh rosemary, chopped      ¼ cup orange juice
1 teaspoon coarse salt                  1 Tbls. Dijon mustard

- ◆ Preheat oven to 350°.
- ◆ In a bowl combine the garlic, rosemary, salt, and pepper. Rub the tenderloin with the mixture and place the roast in an open baking dish. Roast for 1 hour.
- ◆ In a bowl whisk together the cider, orange juice and mustard.
- ◆ Remove the roast and bast with the cider mixture. Cook for ¼ hour more.
- ◆ Remove from oven. Serve on a platter garnished with rosemary sprigs.

# Curried Pork

This is a good way to use leftover pork.

Serves 6-8

¼ cup butter
¼ cup flour
2 cups beef stock
4 cups leftover pork, diced
4 large cloves garlic, minced
1 large apple, peeled, cored and diced
1 medium onion, chopped

1 cup celery, chopped
2 Tbls. curry powder
1 cup seedless raisins
1 teaspoon cayenne
1 teaspoon ground ginger
1 teaspoon cumin
Grated rind of 1 orange

- ◆ In a skillet melt the butter and brown the onions. Add the apples, celery and garlic.
- ◆ Stir in flour and beef stock until thickened. Add pork, raisins, cayenne, ginger, curry, cumin and orange rind.
- ◆ Serve with rice and condiments - chutney, chopped egg, peanuts, fresh coconut, and mashed bananas.

# Veal with Asparagus

Serves 6

2 eggs
¼ cup flour
2 ½ pounds thin veal scallopine
Hollandaise Sauce

½ stick butter
1 pound asparagus

- ◆ In a bowl beat the eggs.
- ◆ Dip the veal in the eggs and then into flour.
- ◆ Melt the butter in a skillet and just brown the veal on each side.
- ◆ Steam the asparagus in a pot of boiling water for 3 minutes.
- ◆ Place the veal on a serving dish, top with the asparagus and hollandaise sauce.
- ◆ This is also very good with fresh crab meat on the veal (otherwise known as Veal Oscar).

# Veal with Tomatoes and Basil

Serves 6

2 eggs, beaten
¼ cup flour
6 6-ounce veal scallops
½ stick butter

4 medium tomatoes, chopped
¼ cup fresh basil, chopped
2 Tbls. olive oil
Salt and pepper, to taste

- Beat the eggs in a bowl.
- Put the flour on a plate. Dip the veal into the eggs and then flour.
- Heat the butter in a skillet. Fry each veal scallopine until golden on each side and cooked through. Drain on paper towels.
- In a bowl combine the tomatoes, basil, salt, pepper and olive oil.
- Serve the tomato mixture over the warmed veal scallops.

# Grilled Veal Chops with Rosemary

Serves 6

6 6-ounce veal chops
½ cup dry white wine
Juice of ½ lemon
2 Tbls. fresh rosemary

4 garlic cloves, minced
1 teaspoon coarse salt
1 teaspoon fresh ground pepper

- Place the veal chops in a shallow baking dish.
- In a bowl combine the wine, lemon juice, rosemary, garlic, salt and pepper. Pour over veal chops. Let marinate overnight in refrigerator.
- Grill the chops. Place on platter. Garnish with lemon slices and fresh rosemary sprigs.
- This is very good using lamb or pork chops, instead of the veal chops.

# Veal with Mushrooms

Serves 6

2 ½ pounds veal scallopine
¼ cup butter
½ pound portabello mushrooms,
sliced

2 shallots, chopped
Parsley
Nutmeg

- Melt the butter in a skillet and saute the mushrooms and shallots. Remove and place in a bowl.
- Brown the veal in the skillet, adding more butter, if necessary. Place the veal on a platter and top with mushrooms.
- Pour sauce over the mushrooms. Garnish with fresh parsley and freshly grated nutmeg.
- Serve hot with spinach noodles or other pasta.

*Cream Sauce*

½ stick butter
¼ cup flour
1½ cups heavy cream

¼ cup Vermouth
Salt and pepper

- In a sauce pan melt the butter and add the flour. Slowly stir in the cream until thickened. Stir in the Vermouth, salt and pepper.

# Beef Nantucket

Serves 6

6 ½-pound beef filets
6 lobster tails

Hollandaise sauce (p. 202)

- Grill the beef filets until desired doneness.
- Grill lobster tails.
- Place beef on a platter and top with the lobster tails and Hollandaise sauce.

*Brie with Cranberry*
*Oysters Rockefeller*
*Beef Tournedoes*
*Garlic Mashed Potatoes*
*Cranberry Salad*
*Green Beans*
*Strawberries Romanoff*

# Beef Tournedoes

Serves 6

2 ½ pounds beef tenderloin            1 red bell pepper, chopped
1 pound crab meat                     6 slices Smithfield ham
1 green pepper, chopped               Bearnaise sauce

- ◆ Grill the beef tenderloin and slice into 6 pieces.
- ◆ Top with a slice of ham, crab meat and sprinkle peppers on top.
- ◆ Pour the Bearnaise sauce over the top.

# Tenderloin with Gorgonzola Port Sauce

Serves 6

2 ½ pounds beef tenderloin

Grill the tenderloin until desired pinkness.

*Gorgonzola Port Sauce*

3 Tbls. butter                        ½ pound Gorgonzola cheese
2 shallots, chopped                   1 cup Port
¼ cup snipped chives

- ◆ In a sauce pan melt the butter and saute the shallots and chives. Stir in the Port and add the cheese. Just slightly melt the cheese.
- ◆ Serve hot in a sauceboat.

# Beef Roulade

Serves 6

2 pounds beef flank steak
½ cup blue cheese
1 pound fresh spinach, stems removed

½ cup pine nuts
2 cloves garlic, minced
Butter

- ♦ Cook the spinach in boiling water until just wilted. Drain thoroughly.
- ♦ In a bowl combine the blue cheese, spinach, nuts and garlic.
- ♦ Slice the steak lengthwise into 3 inch strips.
- ♦ Spread the cheese mixture on the steaks. Roll as tightly as possible. Secure with a toothpick.
- ♦ Melt the butter in a large skillet. Cook beef on each side for about 5 minutes. Serve immediately.
- ♦ The meat can also be baked in a 375° oven for about 15 minutes. However, the cheese has a tendency to melt and drip out.


# Beef Tenderloin with Caramelized Onions, Sauteed Mushrooms and Gorgonzola

Serves 8-10

4 pounds beef tenderloin
1 stick butter
4 large onions, thinly sliced
½ cup sugar

1 pound Portabello mushrooms sliced
1 pound Gorgonzola cheese

- ♦ Grill the beef tenderloin to desired doneness. Place on a platter and slice.
- ♦ In a skillet melt ½ stick of butter and add the onions. Cover and cook for 15 minutes. Sprinkle with the sugar, toss and cook uncovered for 10 minutes. Remove from the skillet.
- ♦ Melt the remaining butter in the skillet and saute the mushrooms.
- ♦ In a sauce pan heat the gorgonzola until just slightly melted.
- ♦ Spoon the mushrooms and onions over the tenderloin.
- ♦ Top with the melted Gorgonzola.

# Beef Oscar

Serves 4

4 filet mignons

1 pound crab meat

1 pound asparagus

Sauce Bearnaise (p. 202)

- In a skillet or sauce pan bring 2 cups of water to a boil and blanch the asparagus for three minutes.
- Grill the filet until desired doneness. Place on a platter.
- Top each filet with asparagus, crab and top with the Bearnaise sauce.


# Venison with Cranberry Sauce

Serves 6

6 venison medallions

Salt and pepper

2 Tbls. olive oil

2 Tbls. butter

- Salt and pepper the venison.
- Heat the olive oil and butter and brown the venison on each side. Remove and place on a platter.

*Sauce*

2 Tbls. red wine

2 Tbls. red wine vinegar

2 cups beef stock

1 bay leaf

1 cup cranberries

¼ cup sugar

Salt and pepper

- Combine all the ingredients in a sauce pan. Bring to a boil, and stir until slightly thickened.
- Serve in a sauceboat with the venison.
- Cranberry sauce can be substituted for the cranberries, just do not add the sugar.

# Vegetables

**Vegetables- Bartlett's Farm Cart, Main Street**

There are several things I do upon arrival on island, other than seeing family and friends. If it's morning and after 9 o'clock, I make a dash to Bartlett's Farm cart on Main Street, a Nantucket institution for over 50 years. Bartlett's owns over 100 acres on Nantucket, but it is their flowers and fresh vegetables that attract so much attention.

# Sauteed Vegetables

Serves 8-10

½ stick butter
1 large head broccoli, chopped
1 summer squash, peeled and sliced
1 large zucchini, peeled and sliced
2 large tomatoes, sliced

1 red bell pepper, sliced
1 green pepper, sliced
1 large onion, sliced
4 cloves garlic, crushed
½ cup fresh basil
Salt and pepper

- Melt the butter in a large skillet. Saute the onions , peppers, garlic and broccoli until just tender. Then add squash and finally tomato and cook until tender.
- Gently stir in the basil. Season with salt and pepper. Serve hot.
- Dill can be substituted for the basil.

# Vegetables in Ranch Dressing

Serves 6-8

1 large head broccoli, chopped
1 large zucchini, peeled and sliced

1 pound mushrooms, sliced
2 Tbls. olive oil
Ranch dressing

- In a large pot bring water to a boil. Cook the broccoli and zucchini for 5 minutes.
- In a skillet with the olive oil, just lightly saute the mushrooms.
- Put the vegetables in a bowl and toss with Ranch Dressing. Add salt and pepper if needed.

# Stir Fried Vegetables

Serves 6

3 cups broccoli florests, chopped
1 pound spinach, no stems
1 large zucchini, sliced
4 scallions, chopped

Sesame oil
Freshly grated pepper
Salt
¼ cup sesame seeds

- ◆ Heat the sesame oil in a wok and stir in vegetables until just tender.
- ◆ Season with salt, pepper and sesame seeds. Serve hot.


# Braised Spinach

Serves 4-6

2 leeks, chopped
½ stick butter
2 pounds spinach, no stems

½ cup pine nuts
½ cup dried cranberries
Zest of 1 lemon

- ◆ Melt the butter in a skillet and saute the leeks.
- ◆ Add the spinach until just wilted.
- ◆ Stir in pine nuts, cranberries and lemon zest. Serve hot.


# Sauteed Spinach

Serves 2

2 Tbls. butter
1 pound spinach
2 shallots finely chopped

1 clove garlic, finely chopped
Salt and pepper
½ teaspoon nutmeg

- ◆ Melt the butter in skillet and saute shallots and garlic. Add spinach.
- ◆ Season with salt, pepper and nutmeg. Serve hot.

# Spinach Torta

1 9" pie crust

3 Tbls. butter
1 pound fresh spinach
½ cup chopped onion
½ cup red bell pepper, chopped
¼ teaspoon nutmeg

4 eggs
2 ½ cups half and half
2 cups mozzarella cheese, shredded

- Preheat oven to 350°.
- Melt the butter in a skillet and saute the onion and pepper. Add the spinach for two minutes.
- In a bowl beat together the eggs, half and half and nutmeg.
- Spoon the spinach, onions and pepper into the pie crust. Spread the mozzarella on top. Pour the egg mixture over the cheese.
- Bake 25 minutes or until set.
- Serve hot or chilled.

# Green Bean and Mushroom Casserole

Serves 8

1 stick butter
1 pound mushrooms, sliced
1 medium onion, chopped
½ cup flour
3 cups half and half
¾ pound grated cheddar cheese
¼ teaspoon Tabasco sauce

2 teaspoons soy sauce
1 teaspoon salt
½ teaspoon pepper
3 pounds green beans
5 oz. can sliced water chestnuts
½ cup toasted slivered almonds

- Preheat the oven to 350°.
- Melt the butter in a skillet and saute the onion and mushrooms. Stir in flour and add half and half. Add the cheese, Tabasco sauce, soy sauce, salt, and pepper. Stir until the cheese is melted.
- Cook the beans in boiling water until just tender. Drain. Place in casserole, and top with water chestnuts.
- Pour the sauce over this. Sprinkle with almonds.
- Bake 30 minutes, or until bubbly.

# Green Bean Casserole

4 servings

1 pound fresh green beans
¼ cup onion, chopped
2 Tbls. butter
2 Tbls. flour

1 teaspoon salt
½ teaspoon pepper
1 cup sour cream
½ cup grated cheddar cheese

- ◆ Preheat oven to 350°.
- ◆ In a skillet melt the butter and add the onion. Add flour, salt, pepper and sour cream.
- ◆ Put the green beans in a casserole. Pour the sauce over the beans. Top with the grated cheese.
- ◆ Bake for 20 minutes, until bubbly.

# Green Beans and Apples

Serves 4

2 Tbls. butter
2 Tbls. water
¼ cup sugar
½ teaspoon salt
¼ teaspoon paprika
4 whole cloves

½ lemon, thinly sliced
1 apple, unpeeled, cored and thinly sliced
1 medium onion, sliced
1 teaspoon cornstarch
1 pound fresh green beans

- ◆ In a sauce pan heat the butter, 2 Tbls. water, sugar, salt, paprika and cloves. Add the lemon slices. Simmer 5 minutes.
- ◆ Stir in the apple and onion slices until just tender. Add cornstarch and stir until thickened.
- ◆ Add beans. Stir until beans are warmed and just tender.
- ◆ Serve hot in a serving bowl.

# Green Beans with Bacon

Serves 4

1 pound green beans
4 slices bacon
¼ cup onion, chopped
¼ cup red sweet pepper, sliced

½ stick butter
¼ cup parsley
Salt and pepper

- ◆ Trim the beans. Place in a large kettle and bring to a boil. Simmer for 5 minutes. Drain and place in a serving dish.
- ◆ Brown the bacon in a skillet. Drain and break into small pieces.
- ◆ Melt the butter in the skillet and add onions and peppers.
- ◆ Toss the onion, peppers and green beans. Sprinkle the bacon over top. Garnish with the parsley. Season with salt and pepper.


# Dilly Green Beans

Serves 6-8

2 pounds green beans
½ teaspoon salt
½ teaspoon fresh ground pepper
½ stick butter

2 cloves garlic, chopped
Juice of ½ lemon
2 Tbls. fresh dill, chopped

- ◆ Cook beans in boiling water for 3-4 minutes, until just tender. Place in a covered serving dish.
- ◆ In a sauce pan melt the butter and saute the garlic. Stir in lemon juice and dill. Pour over green beans. Serve immediately.

# Stuffed Vegetables

Serves 8

1 large zucchini
4 tomatoes
4 red bliss potatoes
1 cup fresh bread crumbs
½ pound sausage
3 cloves garlic, minced

¼ cup onion, chopped
¼ cup fresh basil, chopped
¼ cup parsley
1 cup freshly grated parmesan cheese

- Preheat oven to 350°.
- In a skillet, brown the sausage and onions.
- Slice the zucchini into 1½ inch pieces. Place on a cookie sheet. With a melon baller remove the pulp, grate and place the pulp in the skillet with the sausage.
- Add the parmesan cheese, bread crumbs, garlic, parsley and basil to sausage mixture.
- Cut the potatoes and tomatoes each in half and put on the cookie sheet with the zucchini. Cover the tops of the tomatoes and potatoes with sausage mixture. Stuff the zucchini with the remaining mixture.
- Bake in oven for 30 minutes.
- Remove and place on a platter. Garnish with parsley and basil leaves.
- Ground veal or lamb can be substituted for the sausage.

# Dilly Carrots

Serves 4-6

8 medium carrots, peeled, cut lengthwise in half and sliced

½ stick butter
¼ cup fresh dill, chopped

- In a skillet melt the butter and add carrots. Saute until just tender.
- Add the dill.
- Place on a serving dish and garnish with a sprig of the fresh dill.

# Grilled Vegetables

Serves 12

1 large zucchini, peeled and sliced
1 yellow squash, sliced
8 red bliss potatoes, sliced
1 large eggplant, peeled and sliced
12 cherry tomatoes

1 sweet red pepper, sliced
2 large onions, peeled and sliced
¼ cup fresh rosemary
2 Tbls. coarse salt
1 teaspoon pepper
½ teaspoon cayenne
¼ cup olive oil

- ◆ In a large bowl combine all the vegetables and toss with olive oil, salt, pepper, cayenne and rosemary.
- ◆ Use a hinged wire basket or tin foil for grilling the vegetables. Marinate while cooking so they do not dry out.


# Corn and Vegetable Saute

Serves 6-8

3 slices bacon
1 cup green onions, chopped
4 cups fresh corn
1 large tomato, diced
½ cup yellow pepper, chopped

½ cup green pepper, chopped
½ cup red pepper, chopped
Salt and pepper
¼ teaspoon cayenne

- ◆ In a large skillet cook the bacon until just golden. Remove from pan and add onions, cooking until tender.
- ◆ Add all other ingredients. Simmer for 10 minutes, or until vegetables are tender.
- ◆ Serve immediately.
- ◆ Garnish with fresh parsley and chopped green onions.

# Corn Fritters

2 cups fresh corn
1 teaspoon salt
½ cup milk
2 eggs, beaten

¼ cup green pepper
¼ cup sweet red pepper
1 cup flour
1½ teaspoons baking powder

- ♦ In a bowl combine all the ingredients.
- ♦ Heat 2 Tbls. butter in a skillet.
- ♦ Drop the corn mixture by large spoonfuls into the skillet. Cook until just browned on each side.
- ♦ For a spicier taste add 1 green chilie, seeded and chopped finely and ¼ cup fresh cilantro.
- ♦ These are good served with salsa or maple syrup.

# Minted Cucumbers

- ♦ Serve with a spicy chicken, lamb or seafood entrée.

Serves 4

2 cucumbers, sliced thinly
1 teaspoon salt
¼ cup fresh mint, chopped

1 clove garlic, crushed
½ cup sour cream

- ♦ Combine all the ingredients in a bowl.

# Cucumber and Dill

Serves 4

2 cucumbers, sliced thinly
2 Tbls. chives, snipped
2 Tbls. dill, chopped

¾ cup sour cream
Salt and pepper

- Place the cucumbers in a bowl and salt. Refrigerate covered for at least two hours.
- Combine with the other ingredients and serve immediately.
- Serve with salmon or other fresh seafood.

# Onion Tagine

Serve this with grilled meats

Serves 4

4 large red onions, sliced very thin
½ cup olive oil
Pinch of saffron

½ teaspoon ground ginger
1 teaspoon black pepper
1 teaspoon ground cinnamon
1 Tbls. sugar

- Preheat the oven to 325°.
- In a casserole combine the olive oil, saffron, ginger, pepper, cinnamon and sugar. Stir in the onions. Cover.
- Bake for 45 minutes.
- Remove cover and bake for 10 minutes at 400°. Serve hot.

# Orange Turnips

Serves 4

½ stick butter
1 shallot, chopped
1 pound turnips, peeled and
quartered

1 cup fresh orange juice
½ cup slivered almonds
Salt and pepper

- Melt the butter in a skillet and add the shallot. Cook until just tender.
- Add the turnips. Pour the orange juice over the turnips. Simmer 30 minutes.
- Season with salt and pepper.
- Pour into a serving bowl and garnish with almonds.

# Peas and Mushrooms with Rice

Serves 8

1 pound fresh peas
2 cups basmati rice
½ pound mushrooms, sliced
2 garlic cloves, crushed
4 whole cloves
1 small onion, chopped

1 teaspoon salt
1 large tomato, chopped
½ teaspoon ground tumeric
1 teaspoon ground cumin
3 cups chicken stock
2 Tbls. olive oil

- Heat the oil in a sauce pan and add onion and garlic.
- Stir in the cloves, salt, tumeric and cumin.
- Add the rice, peas, mushrooms, and tomato.
- Pour in the chicken stock. Bring to a boil and simmer for 20 minutes, or until all the liquid is absorbed.

# Potato Spinach Croquettes

Serves 6

1 lb. red bliss potatoes, peeled
½ teaspoon nutmeg
½ cup freshly grated parmesan cheese
1 cup cooked fresh spinach
¼ cup onion, chopped

½ cup flour
3 eggs, beaten
1½ cups fresh bread crumbs
1 teaspoon salt
½ teaspoon pepper
Oil for cooking

- In a saucepan boil the potatoes for 20 minutes. Drain. Mash the potatoes.
- In a bowl combine the parmesan cheese, onion and spinach. Add the potatoes, nutmeg, salt and pepper.
- On a floured surface roll the mixture into cylinder or ball shapes.
- Put the flour on a plate and the bread crumbs on a piece of waxed paper. Roll the croquettes in the flour, then dip them into the beaten eggs, draining off any excess egg. Roll them in the bread crumbs.
- In a skillet heat the oil until bubbly, but not smoking. Fry in batches, draining off any excess oil. Drain on paper towels.
- Serve immediately.

# Red Bliss Potatoes with Caviar

This can be used as an appetizer or side dish.

Serves 8-10

16 small red bliss potatoes
¼ cup olive oil
1 Tbls. coarse salt

½ cup sour cream
4 ounces black caviar
16 basil leaves

- In a large pan boil the potatoes until tender. Drain.
- Cut the potatoes in half. Drizzle with a small amount of olive oil.
- Cover each potato with a dollop of sour cream. Top with caviar. Garnish with basil leaf.

# Crab Stuffed Baked Potatoes

Serves 4

4 large baking potatoes
½ pound crab meat
½ stick butter
½ cup half and half
½ teaspoon salt

½ teaspoon pepper
Dash of cayenne or Old Bay
Seasoning
1 scallion, chopped

- ♦ Preheat oven to 350°.
- ♦ Scrub the potatoes and bake in oven until tender, about 1 hour.
- ♦ Remove the potatoes and cut in half. Remove the pulp and place in a bowl. Reserve the skins. Beat together the potatoes, butter, half and half, salt, pepper, scallions and cayenne. Carefully fold in the crab meat.
- ♦ Stuff the potato skins with the crab mixture.
- ♦ Bake in oven for 15 minutes until just browned, or place under broiler.
- ♦ ½ cup cheddar cheese may be added to the mixture.
- ♦ Bacon, clams, or ham can be substituted for the crab meat.

# Garlic Mashed Potatoes

Serves 6

8 red bliss potatoes
3 cloves garlic, minced
½ cup sour cream

½ stick butter
Salt and pepper

- ♦ Cook the potatoes in boiling water until tender. Drain.
- ♦ In a bowl combine the potatoes, garlic, sour cream, butter, salt and pepper. Beat until well blended.
- ♦ Serve immediately.

# Garlic Potato Cakes

- ♦ Use the recipe for Garlic Mashed Potatoes above.
- ♦ Shape the mashed potatoes into patties the size of a silver dollar.
- ♦ Melt the butter in a skillet and brown the patties on each side.
- ♦ Serve immediately with a dollop of sour cream and chives.
- ♦ 1 leek, chopped, can be added to the recipe for more flavor.

# Blue Cheese Mashed Potatoes

Serves 6-8

8 large red bliss potatoes
½ cup half and half
½ stick butter

¼ pound blue cheese or Gorgonzola
Salt and pepper

- ♦ Cook the potatoes in boiling water until tender. Drain.
- ♦ In a bowl beat the potatoes with the other ingredients.
- ♦ Serve immediately.

# Potatoes au Gratin

Serves 6-8

2 lbs. potatoes, peeled and cut into thin slices
½ stick butter
1 teaspoon salt
Fresh ground pepper

½ pound Gruyere cheese, grated
2 Tbls. fresh parsley, chopped
2 Tbls. fresh chives, snipped
1 small onion, chopped
2 cups half and half

- ♦ Preheat the oven to 350°.
- ♦ Line a buttered 9" x 13" baking dish with the potatoes. Dot with butter and sprinkle with other ingredients. Pour the half and half over the potatoes.
- ♦ Cover with tin foil and bake 1 hour.

# Sweet Potato Casserole

Serves 6-8

6 large sweet potatoes, peeled
and cubed
½ cup brown sugar
½ stick butter
1 egg, beaten

1 teaspoon cinnamon
¼ teaspoon nutmeg
¼ teaspoon ginger
½ cup milk

- Preheat oven to 350°.
- Cook potatoes in boiling water until tender.
- Mash potatoes with all the ingredients. Spoon into a greased casserole dish. Bake 25-30 minutes or until golden brown.

*Topping*

2 Tbls. butter
¼ cup brown sugar

1 cup pecans

- Combine ingredients and sprinkle on top of sweet potatoes.

# Courge Squash

Serves 6-8

4 cups courge squash, peeled
and grated
1 onion, chopped
2 Tbls. butter
2 garlic cloves, crushed
1 green pepper, chopped

1 red bell pepper, chopped
¼ cup fresh basil, chopped
1 Tbls. soy sauce
¼ cup freshly grated parmesan
cheese

- Preheat oven to 350°.
- Melt the butter in a skillet and saute onion and peppers until tender. Add garlic.
- Stir in the squash, soy and basil. Sprinkle the parmesan cheese on top.
- Cook for 15 minutes. Serve immediately.

# Asparagus Tart

½ pound asparagus, trimmed
and cut in 1" pieces
4 large eggs
1 cups half and half

2 Tbls. butter
½ teaspoon salt
½ pound Gruyere cheese, sliced

- ♦ Preheat the oven to 350°.
- ♦ Place the asparagus in a pot of boiling water for 3 minutes. Drain and pat dry.
- ♦ Arrange the asparagus in the bottom of the pie crust. Top with cheese.
- ♦ In a bowl combine the half and half and eggs. Pour over the cheese.
- ♦ Bake 45 minutes or until set. Serve warm or chilled.

*Pie Crust*

1 ¼ cups flour
1 stick butter

½ teaspoon salt
¼ cup water

- ♦ In a food processor combine all ingredients until a ball forms. Roll out on a floured board into the shape of a pie plate.

# Stewed Tomatoes

Serves 4

4 large tomatoes, chopped
½ cup butter

¾ cup sugar
¼ cup fresh basil leaves

- ♦ Bring all the ingredients to a boil in a sauce pan.
- ♦ Reduce heat and simmer for 1 hour or until thickened.
- ♦ Serve hot.

# Scalloped Tomatoes

Serves 6-8

1 large red sweet pepper, diced
4 large tomatoes, sliced
1 teaspoon salt
½ teaspoon pepper
1 cup bread crumbs

1 cup fresh grated parmesan
cheese
½ cup olive oil
½ cup fresh basil leaves

- In a greased baking dish sprinkle ¼ cup bread crumbs and top with ½ the tomatoes and ¼ cup cheese. Sprinkle with salt and pepper.
- Repeat layer.
- Top with rest of bread crumbs, cheese and sliced pepper.
- Sprinkle with basil leaves and drizzle with oil.
- Bake 30 minutes. Serve immediately.
- 1 Tbls. thyme can be substituted for the basil leaves.


# Tomato Broccoli Delight

Serves 6

1 pound broccoli (head), chopped
3 large tomatoes, halved
1 teaspoon salt

1 cup fresh parmesan cheese
¼ cup onion
½ teaspoon fresh ground pepper

- Preheat broiler.
- Cook the broccoli in boiling water until just tender. Drain.
- Place the tomatoes on a baking sheet and sprinkle with salt.
- In a food processor combine the broccoli, cheese, onion and pepper. Just blend until broccoli is finely chopped. Spread mixture on the tomatoes.
- Broil until just browned.
- Fresh spinach can be substituted for the broccoli.

# Tomato Pudding

Serves 4

¾ cup brown sugar
10 ounce can tomato puree
½ teaspoon salt

1 cup diced bread
½ cup melted butter

- Preheat oven to 350°.
- Combine the sugar, salt and tomato puree in a saucepan and heat for 5 minutes.
- Put the bread in a casserole dish. Top with butter.
- Pour the tomato mixture over the bread.
- Bake for 30 minutes.

# Tomato Tart

Serves 4

*Pastry shell*

1 ¼ cups flour
1 stick butter

¼ cup water
3 Tbls. cream cheese

- Place all the ingredients in a food processor until a ball forms. Roll out on a floured board in the shape of 9" pie. Place in pie plate.

*Filling*

4 large tomatoes, sliced
2 cups mozzarella cheese, shredded
½ cup mayonnaise

¼ cup grated parmesan cheese
2 cloves garlic, minced
¼ cup fresh basil
2 Tbls. olive oil

- Preheat oven to 375°.
- Sprinkle bottom of pie plate with 1 cup mozzarella. Arrange the tomato slices over the cheese.
- In a bowl combine 1 cup mozzarella, mayonnaise, parmesan cheese, garlic, basil and olive oil. Spread over tomato slices.
- Bake 25-25 minutes until crust is just browned.

# Broccoli au Gratin

Serves 4-6

12 small white onions, peeled
½ stick butter
¼ cup flour
1 cup half and half

½ cup freshly grated parmesan
cheese
Salt and pepper
¼ teaspoon nutmeg
1 large bunch broccoli, chopped

- Preheat broiler.
- In a sauce pan melt the butter and saute onions until just tender. Add the flour, then half and half until thickened. Add salt and pepper to taste, and nutmeg.
- Add the broccoli, and cook for about 10 minutes.
- Place mixture in a baking dish and cover with grated parmesan cheese.
- Place under broiler until just browned.

# Roasted Peppers

Serves 4

1 red sweet pepper
1 green pepper
1 yellow pepper

¼ cup fresh basil leaves
Salt and pepper to taste
¼ cup olive oil

- Preheat oven to 375°.
- Cut the peppers into strips removing the seed and membranes.
- Pour the oil into an oven proof skillet and place the peppers in the skillet. Cook for 30 minutes, just browned and tender. Remove from oven and stir in basil, salt and pepper.
- Serve as a side dish.

# Braised Red Cabbage

Serves 8

1 large head red cabbage
¼ cup butter
1 large onion, sliced
2 apples, peeled, cored and
·sliced

¼ cup white wine vinegar
2 Tbls. flour
1 teaspoon mustard seed

- ◆ Preheat the oven to 325°.
- ◆ Quarter the cabbage and discard the stalk. Chop the cabbage finely.
- ◆ In a large pot place the cabbage and add enough water to cover the cabbage. Bring to a boil. Drain.
- ◆ Melt 1 Tbls. butter in a Dutch oven. Add the onion and cook until transparent.
- ◆ Add the apples, cabbage, vinegar, sugar, and mustard seed. Cover with the lid and bake 1½ hours, stirring occasionally.
- ◆ Remove from oven. Stir in the remaining butter and flour to thicken.
- ◆ Serve hot.

# Ratatoille

Serves 8-10

1 large onion, chopped
4 large tomatoes, chopped
3 cloves garlic, minced
1 sweet red pepper, sliced thinly
1 large zucchini, sliced

2 medium eggplant, sliced
1 cup basil, chopped
Salt and pepper
Bouquet garni
Olive oil

- ◆ Preheat oven to 350°.
- ◆ In a Dutch oven cook the onion in 2 Tbls. olive oil, until transparent. Add the tomato, red pepper, salt, pepper and garlic and cook for 15 minutes.
- ◆ In a skillet saute the zucchini and eggplant in olive oil. Add to the tomato mixture, along with the bouquet garni. Cover and bake for 30 minutes. Stir in the basil leaves.
- ◆ Serve hot or cold.

# Eggplant Casserole

Serves 8

2 medium eggplant
4 cloves garlic, crushed
2 bunches basil, stems removed
and chopped
¼ cup olive oil

4 large tomatoes, sliced thinly
½ cup fresh grated parmesan
cheese
2 Tbls. fresh parsley, chopped
Salt and pepper

- ◆ Preheat oven to 400°.
- ◆ Cut the stems from the eggplant and slice. Place in a baking dish and cover with garlic and 2 Tbls. olive oil. Cover with tin foil. Bake for 20 minutes. Remove from oven.
- ◆ Sprinkle with lemon juice and top with tomatoes, basil, parmesan cheese, and remaining olive oil.
- ◆ Cover with foil and bake for 20 minutes.
- ◆ Serve immediately, garnished with parsley.

# Salads

**Salad and Nantucket Basket at the Barnacle**

# Curried Lobster Salad

Serves 8

3 pounds lobster meat
1 cup mayonnaise
1 Tbls. curry powder
½ cup celery, chopped

½ cup green onion, chopped
1 cucumber, peeled and diced
Juice of 1 lemon
1 teaspoon fresh grated ginger

- In a bowl combine all the ingredients except for lobster.
- Gently fold in lobster.
- Serve salad on a bed of mixed spring greens, garnished with quartered hardboiled eggs, sliced tomato, and cucumber slices.
- For variety add ½ cup chutney to the salad, or serve in a side bowl.

# Lobster Salad

Serves 4

1½ pounds fresh lobster meat
½ cup celery, chopped
2 green onions, chopped
2 Tbls. fresh tarragon

½ cup mayonnaise
Juice of 1 lemon
1 Tbls Dijon mustard
1 Tbls. capers

- In a bowl combine all the ingredients, except lobster.
- Fold in the lobster.
- Serve on a bed of mixed spring greens, and garnish with cherry tomatoes, sliced cucumber and fresh basil leaves.

# Lobster and Potato Salad

Serves 4

1 pound lobster meat
1 pound small red bliss potatoes, cubed
1 cup celery, chopped
2 green onions, chopped
¼ cup basil

½ cup mayonnaise
Juice of 1 lemon
Salt and pepper, to taste
4 hardboiled eggs
1 large tomato, sliced
1 cucumber, thinly sliced

- ♦ In a pan cook the potatoes until tender. Drain.
- ♦ In a bowl combine the potatoes, celery, onions, basil, mayonnaise, lemon juice, salt and pepper..
- ♦ Serve on individual plates. Garnish with tomato slices, cucumber slices and hardboiled eggs quartered.

# Salmon, Shrimp and Crab Salad

Serves 6

1 pound shrimp, deveined and cooked
1 pound fresh crab meat
1 pound smoked salmon, broken up into small pieces

1 cup mayonnaise
¼ cup fresh basil
Juice of 1 lemon

- ♦ In a bowl combine all the ingredients.

Romaine lettuce
2 tomatoes, sliced
1 red onion, sliced
1 cucumber, sliced

1 package bean sprouts
6 hardboiled sliced eggs
1 cup shredded cheddar cheese

- ♦ On a serving platter arrange the romaine leaves and spoon the seafood salad on top.
- ♦ Around the edge of the platter arrange the tomatoes, onion, cucumber and eggs.
- ♦ Sprinkle the sprouts and grated cheese over the salad.

**Dinner on the Porch**

*Seafood Salad*
*Hot Portuguese Rolls*
*Fresh Fruit and Cheese*

# Seafood Salad

Serves 8-10

1 pound smoked salmon
1 pound fresh tuna, grilled
1 pound shrimp, deveined and cooked
1 pound fresh crab meat
1 pound smoked scallops

1 pound Roma tomatoes, sliced
14½ ounce can artichoke hearts, quartered
1 cup hazelnuts
Romaine lettuce

- ◆ In a bowl combine the seafood with the dressing.
- ◆ In a salad bowl or seafood platter arrange the lettuce and spoon the salad over the leaves. Pour the hot vinaigrette dressing on top.
- ◆ Garnish with the tomatoes, artichoke hearts and hazelnuts.

*Hot Vinaigrette Dressing*

½ cup olive oil
2 medium shallots, chopped
½ cup dry white wine
¼ cup fresh basil

¼ cup fresh parsley
2 cloves garlic, crushed
Salt and pepper, to taste

- ◆ In a skillet heat the oil and saute the shallots and garlic. Stir in the other ingredients.

**Lady's Luncheon**

*Shrimp Salad*
*Brie*
*Fresh Vegetable Platter*
*Assorted Breads*
*Strawberries Dipped in Chocolate*

# Shrimp Salad

Serves 8

2 pounds medium shrimp
½ pound snow peas
2 green onions, chopped
1 green pepper, chopped
½ cup fresh basil
¾ cup mayonnaise

Juice of 1 lemon
3 large tomatoes, sliced
8 hardboiled eggs, quartered
1 pound fresh thin asparagus
1 cucumber sliced
Mixed spring salad greens

- In a large salad bowl combine the shrimp, snow peas, green onions, pepper, ¼ cup basil, mayonnaise and lemon juice. Garnish with one egg and basil leaves.
- On a platter arrange the mixed greens, then circle the platter alternating the tomatoes, cucumber and sliced eggs. Fan out the asparagus at each end.
- If you have a very large platter you can arrange the spring greens first, top with the shrimp salad and garnish with the eggs, tomatoes, cucumber and asparagus.

# Scallop Salad

Serves 4

2 pounds bay scallops, grilled
4 medium red bliss potatoes
1 celery stalk, chopped
¼ cup red onion, chopped

2 Tbls. olive oil
2 Tbls. fresh lime juice
½ pound mixed spring greens
Salt and pepper

- Boil the potatoes until just tender. Drain. Quarter.
- Toss the potatoes with the rest of the ingredients, except spring greens in a bowl.
- Divide up the spring greens among the 4 plates. Spoon the scallops on top.

# Grilled Salmon Salad

Serves 4

2 pounds salmon
¼ cup fresh lemon juice
2 Tbls. olive oil
4 large red bliss potatoes, cubed

1 pound thin asparagus
1 green onion, chopped
1 pint grape tomatoes
½ pound spring greens

- In a flat dish coat the salmon with lemon juice and olive oil. Grill until desired pinkness.
- In a pan boil the potatoes until almost tender. Add the asparagus for 3 minutes.
- On a platter arrange the spring greens and top with salmon.
- Garnish with asparagus, green onion and tomatoes. Drizzle the pesto sauce over the salad.

*Lemon Pesto*

4 cloves garlic
1 large bunch basil leaves,
without stems
½ cup pine nuts

½ cup grated parmesan cheese
¼ cup olive oil
¼ cup fresh lemon juice

- Combine all ingredients in a food processor.

# Hot Steak Salad

Serves 6

2 ½ pounds tenderloin
½ pound mixed spring salad greens

6 red bell peppers

- Preheat oven to 400°.
- Place the peppers on a cookie sheet and prick each with a fork. Bake 25 minutes. Remove and cut into quarters, removing seeds and membrane.
- Grill the tenderloin on a grill until desired pinkness.
- Arrange the spring greens on a serving platter. Arrange tenderloin on top and then roasted peppers.
- Serve with horseradish dressing.

*Horseradish Dressing*

1 cup heavy cream
1 cup mayonnaise
½ teaspoon salt

¼ cup horseradish
½ teaspoon fresh ground black pepper

- Whip the cream in a bowl until stiff.
- Beat in mayonnaise, salt, pepper and horseradish.

# Oriental Chicken Salad

Serves 8

4 cups cooked chicken, diced
8 ounce package cream cheese
½ cup mayonnaise
½ cup raisins
½ cup coconut, toasted

1 cup celery, finely chopped
3 scallions, chopped
1 cup slivered almonds, toasted
2 Tbls. curry powder
2 Tbls. fresh ginger, grated

- In a bowl combine all the ingredients.
- Cover and refrigerate for 2 hours.
- Serve on a bed of lettuce with chutney as an accompaniment.

# Chicken Salad

Serves 4-6

4 cups cooked chicken, diced
1 cup celery, chopped
1 cucumber, peeled and chopped
1 red bell pepper, sliced

4 green onions, chopped
½ cup peanuts
2 large tomatoes, chopped
1 small red onion, sliced

♦ In a bowl toss all the ingredients.

*Dressing*

½ cup sour cream
½ cup mango chutney
1 Tbls. grated orange rind

1 teaspoon fresh lemon juice
½ teaspoon curry powder

♦ In a bowl combine all the ingredients. Toss with the salad.

# Chicken Breast Salad

Serves 6

6 chicken breasts
2 apples, cored and sliced

1 cup walnuts
1 lb.mixed spring salad greens

♦ Grill chicken on a BBQ until desired doneness.
♦ On 6 salad plates arrange the mixed spring greens.
♦ Place the chicken on top.
♦ Garnish with the apples and walnut.
♦ Sprinkle with the vinaigrette.

*Raspberry Vinaigrette*

¼ cup raspberry vinegar
¼ cup olive oil

2 Tbls. raspberry jam

♦ In a bowl combine the ingredients.

# Ham Mousse

Serves 4

½ cup chicken stock
2 eggs, separated
1 cup heavy cream, whipped
2 cups cooked ham, chopped
1 Tbls. tomato paste

2 Tbls. Madeira
1 teaspoon horseradish
1 tbls. Dijon mustard
1 envelope plain gelatin

- Bring the chicken stock to a boil in a sauce pan. Stir in the gelatin to dissolve.
- In a bowl beat the egg yolks, add a little gelatin, and slowly stir into gelatin. Cook over low heat, stirring with a wooden spoon until sauce coats the spoon. Cool.
- Beat the egg whites until stiff. Beat the cream until stiff and fold into egg whites. Fold in ham and other ingredients.
- Pour into a quart and half mold. Chill.
- Unmold onto a platter arranged with lettuce. Garnish with parsley.

# Caesar Salad

Serves 6

1 large head romaine lettuce
3 cloves garlic, crushed
Juice of one lemon
1 cup fresh croutons
1 can anchovies

1 egg
¼ cup freshly grated parmesan cheese
¼ cup olive oil
Salt and pepper

- Rub the crushed garlic around the sides of a large salad bowl. Add salt and pepper, lemon juice and olive oil.
- Tear the lettuce into bite-size pieces and add to the bowl.
- Add the anchovies and break an egg over the salad.
- Sprinkle the croutons on top and then the grated cheese.
- Serve immediately.
- This is good with grilled swordfish, scallops, grilled tenderloin, or chicken on top.

# Salade Nicoise

Serves 4

1½ pounds fresh tuna
4 medium red bliss potatoes, cut in quarters
½ pound green beans
1 red sweet pepper, cut in julienne strips
1 large red onion, sliced thinly
2 large tomatoes, cut in wedges
1 head Boston lettuce

4 hard-cooked eggs, peeled and quartered
1 can anchovy filets
12 black olives
½ cup olive oil
¼ cup red wine vinegar
¼ fresh basil
Salt and pepper

- ◆ Grill or broil the tuna. Break into small pieces.
- ◆ In a pan boil the potatoes until tender.
- ◆ Trim the beans and boil for 4 minutes.
- ◆ In a bowl make the vinaigrette by whisking together the oil and vinegar. Add the basil, salt and pepper.
- ◆ In a bowl toss the potatoes, green beans, red pepper, and tuna with ½ the vinaigrette.
- ◆ Arrange the lettuce leaves on 4 plates. In the center place the tuna mixture.
- ◆ Alternate the eggs and tomatoes around the edge. Top with the anchovies and olives.
- ◆ Drizzle the remaining vinaigrette over the salad.
- ◆ Serve with warm bread.
- ◆ A meal in itself!

# Cole Slaw

Serves 8

1 large head cabbage, sliced very
thin
2 green onions, sliced
2 carrots, peeled and grated
1 teaspoon celery seed
¼ cup vegetable oil

½ cup cider vinegar
½ cup sugar
1 teaspoon salt
½ teaspoon pepper
Pinch of cayenne

- ♦ In a salad bowl combine the cabbage, onions, carrots and celery seed.
- ♦ In a sauce pan heat the vegetable oil, vinegar, sugar, salt and pepper
  to boiling. Pour over the salad and toss.

# Orange and Spinach Salad

Serves 4

1 pound baby spinach
2 fresh oranges, sliced

1 cup pecans or almonds
1 large red onion

- ♦ In a salad bowl combine all the ingredients.
- ♦ Spiced pecans can be substituted for the pecans for a different flavor.

*Balsamic Vinaigrette*

2 Tbls. balsamic vinegar
2 Tbls. olive oil

2 Tbls. lemon juice
2 Tbls. honey

- ♦ Combine the ingredients in a bowl and pour over salad.

# Cheese and Nut Spinach Salad

Serves 6

1 pound fresh spinach, washed and stems removed
½ pound endive
2 apples, sliced

½ pound Gorgonzola cheese, crumbled
1 cup walnuts
1 small red onion, sliced

- ◆ Combine the spinach and endive in a salad bowl.
- ◆ Arrange the apples and onion slices on top.
- ◆ Sprinkle the Gorgonzola and nuts on top.

*Dressing*

¼ cup olive oil
¼ cup balsamic vinegar
2 Tbls. honey

2 Tbls. lemon juice
1 Tbls. Dijon mustard

- ◆ Combine all the ingredients in a bowl and pour over salad.

# Raspberry Spinach Salad

Serves 8

2 pounds spinach, washed and stems removed

1 cup walnuts
2 cups fresh raspberries

- ◆ In a large salad bowl toss the spinach with the dressing.
- ◆ Add the walnuts and raspberries.
- ◆ Serve immediately.

*Dressing*

¼ cup raspberry vinegar
¼ cup olive oil

2 Tbls. raspberry jam

- ◆ In a bowl combine the raspberry vinegar, olive oil, and jam.

# Spinach Salad

Serves 6

1 pound fresh spinach, washed and stems removed
½ pound Gorgonzola cheese, crumbled
6 slices bacon, cooked

3 hardboiled eggs, sliced
1 small red onion, sliced
½ pound mushrooms, sliced
1 cup fresh bread croutons

♦ In a large salad bowl combine the ingredients.

*Hot Bacon Dressing*

Fat from bacon, still hot
¼ cup red wine vinegar
1 Tbls. sugar

Salt and pepper
½ teaspoon dry mustard

♦ In a jar combine all the ingredients. Pour over the salad and toss salad.

# Baby Beet Salad

Serves 8

1 lb. mixed spring salad greens
½ pound mushrooms, sliced
2 carrots, peeled and grated

1 cucumber, peeled and sliced
2 bunches baby beets, no tops

♦ In a pan boil the beets until tender. Peel skins and leave the beets whole.
♦ Combine the ingredients in a salad bowl.

*Dressing*

¼ cup olive oil
¼ cup balsamic vinegar

2 Tbls. sesame seeds
Juice of 1 lemon

♦ In a bowl combine the ingredients. Pour over the salad and toss.

# Beet Salad

Serves 6

1 large bunch beets
1 pound arugala

2 oranges, peeled and sliced
½ pound Roquefort cheese

- ♦ Cook the beets until tender. Peel and thinly slice.
- ♦ Arrange the arugala in a salad bowl.
- ♦ Arrange the beets and orange slices in a circle.
- ♦ Sprinkle cheese over the beets.

*Dressing*

2 Tbls. olive oil
2 Tbls. balsamic vinegar

2 Tbls. honey
¼ cup orange juice

- ♦ Combine all the ingredients in a bowl. Toss with the salad.

# Summer Salad

Serves 6-8

1 lb. mixed spring salad greens
1 cup roasted walnuts
1 large red onion, sliced
1 cucumber, peeled and sliced
1 cup black olives

½ pound feta cheese, crumbled
¼ cup balsamic vinegar
¼ cup olive oil
Salt and pepper

- ♦ In a large salad bowl combine the spring greens, walnuts, red onion, cucumber and olives.
- ♦ Sprinkle the feta over the salad.
- ♦ In a bowl combine the olive oil, vinegar, salt and pepper.
- ♦ Pour over the salad and toss.

# Watercress Salad

Serves 8

2 large bunches watercress
½ pound fresh spinach
½ head red leaf lettuce
2 oranges, peeled and segmented

1 cup sliced almonds, toasted
1 avocado, peeled, pitted, and sliced

- ♦ Wash the watercress, spinach and lettuce, discarding stems. Arrange in a salad bowl.
- ♦ Decorate with orange segments, almonds and avocado.
- ♦ Pour the vinaigrette over the salad.

*Vinaigrette*

½ cup olive oil
¼ cup cider vinegar
Juice of 1 orange

Juice of 1 lemon
Juice of 1 lime
Salt and Pepper

- ♦ Combine all the ingredients in a bowl or jar. Chill until ready to use.


# Mixed Greens Salad

Serves 8

1 lb. mixed spring salad greens
1 cup blue cheese, crumbled
1 cup dried cranberries
1 cup pecans

¼ cup balsamic vinegar
¼ cup olive oil
2 Tbls. lemon juice
2 Tbls. honey

- ♦ In a salad bowl toss together the spring greens, blue cheese, cranberries and pecans.
- ♦ In a bowl combine the vinegar, olive oil, lemon juice and honey. Pour over the salad and toss.

# Country Salad

Serves 8

1 lb. mixed spring salad greens
½ pound smoked bacon, cooked and crumbled
1 cup French bread croutons

1 Vidalia onion, chopped
1 large bunch fresh beets, no tops

- ♦ In a pan boil the beets until tender. Peel and slice.
- ♦ In a bowl combine the mixed spring salad greens, bacon, croutons, onion and beets.

*Dressing*

2 teaspoons horseradish
2 Tbls. lemon juice

¼ cup red wine vinegar
¼ cup olive oil

- ♦ Combine ingredients in a bowl.
- ♦ Pour over the salad and toss.

# Asparagus Salad

8 servings

1½ pounds thin asparagus
¼ cup white wine vinegar
½ cup olive oil
¼ cup honey
2 cloves garlic, minced

1 apple, thinly sliced
¼ pound sharp white cheddar cheese, thinly sliced
1 pound mixed spring greens

- ♦ Preheat the oven to 400°.
- ♦ Place the asparagus on a cookie sheet and sprinkle with at least 2 tablespoons of the olive oil. Roast in oven for 25 minutes. Let cool.
- ♦ In a jar combine the olive oil, vinegar, honey and garlic. Shake well.
- ♦ On a platter or in a salad bowl arrange the salad greens. Top with the apple slices and cheese, then the asparagus.
- ♦ When ready to serve pour the salad dressing over the asparagus.
- ♦ I use about half this dressing, and save enough for another salad.

# Cranberry Salad

1 envelope unflavored gelatin
½ cup sugar
¼ teaspoon salt
1 cup water
½ cup mayonnaise

2 Tbls. lemon juice
1 Tbls. grated lemon rind
1 pound cranberries
½ cup walnuts, chopped

- ♦ In a sauce pan combine the gelatin, sugar, salt and water. Dissolve over low heat. Remove from heat. Cool.
- ♦ Add mayonnaise, lemon juice and lemon rind. Refrigerate for 15 minutes.
- ♦ Beat until fluffy. Fold in cranberries and nuts. Turn into a mold. Refrigerate.
- ♦ Unmold onto a plate with lettuce. Garnish with cranberries. Serve with mayonnaise.
- ♦ 1 can whole cranberry sauce can be substituted for the fresh cranberries. Use only 2 Tbls. sugar.

# Cranberry Nut Salad

4 cups cranberries
2 cups water
1½ cups sugar
2 envelopes plain gelatin
½ cup hot water

½ cup apples, peeled, cored and chopped
½ cup celery, thinly sliced
½ cup pecans or walnuts

- ♦ In a sauce pan bring the cranberries, 2 cups water and sugar to a boil. Remove from heat.
- ♦ Dissolve the gelatin in the hot water. Stir into cranberries. Cool.
- ♦ Add apples, celery, and nuts. Pour into a mold and chill.
- ♦ Unmold onto a platter with a bed of lettuce.
- ♦ Serve with a bowl of mayonnaise or sour cream.
- ♦ Small cream cheese balls can be added with the apples, celery and pecans for color.

# Tomatoes with Mozzarella

Serves 8

½ pound fresh mozzarella, sliced
4 large tomatoes, halved
1 teaspoon salt
1 teaspoon fresh ground pepper

1 cup fresh basil leaves
¼ cup olive oil
¼ cup balsamic vinegar
3 garlic cloves, minced
1 teaspoon sugar

- In a bowl combine the olive oil, vinegar, garlic and sugar.
- On separate plates place a tomato half, sprinkle with salt and pepper, top with mozzarella and two basil leaves.
- Drizzle the oil dressing over top.
- Serve as a side dish.
- This is also very good placed under the broiler until the mozzarella starts to melt.

# Tomato and Bread Salad

Serves 4

½ loaf French bread
4 medium tomatoes, peeled, seeded and chopped
1 red onion, chopped
½ cup chicken stock

2 cloves garlic, minced
¼ cup fresh basil, chopped
¼ cup olive oil
Salt and pepper

- Heat the olive oil in a large sauce pan. Saute the onions and the garlic. Add the tomatoes, basil, stock, salt and pepper. Simmer for 15 minutes.
- Tear or cut the bread into small pieces. Add to tomatoes and cook for 1 minute.
- Serve at room temperature. Garnish with the basil.

# Corn Salad

Serves 8

4 cups cooked fresh corn
1 cup red onion, chopped
2 large tomatoes, chopped
1 red bell pepper, chopped
1 green pepper, chopped
½ teaspoon coarse salt

½ teaspoon fresh ground pepper
1 green jalapeno, seeded and chopped
¼ cup olive oil
2 Tbls. red wine vinegar

- ◆ In a bowl combine all ingredients. Refrigerate.
- ◆ Serve as a side dish.


# Cucumber Salad

Serves 4

1 large cucumber, thinly sliced
¼ cup green pepper, chopped
1 green onion, chopped
2 Tbls. fresh tarragon
2 Tbls. fresh dill

1 Tbls. lemon juice
¼ teaspoon salt
1 cup sour cream
2 Tbls. white wine vinegar

- ◆ In a bowl combine all the ingredients. Refrigerate for at least one hour before serving.
- ◆ Serve as a side dish. Good with spicy food, such as Indian curries.

# *Pastas and Rice*

**Nantucket Harbor**

# Seafood Pasta

Serves 6

2 dozen mussels, in shell washed and scrubbed
2 dozen littleneck clams
1 pound scallops
1 cup dry white wine
4 cloves garlic, minced

½ teaspoon crushed red pepper
¼ cup olive oil
1 pound fettuccine
¼ cup parsley, chopped
Salt and pepper

- In a large pot bring the wine to boil. Add the mussels and clams until opened. Add scallops for 3 minutes. Remove pot from the heat. Use tongs to remove the shellfish. Reserve liquor.
- In a large sauce pan heat the olive oil and add the garlic. Cook for 2 minutes. Add red pepper, reserved liquor and shellfish.
- Cook the fettuccine according to the directions. Drain. Place in large serving bowl or individual bowls.
- Pour the seafood mixture over the fettuccine. Season with salt and pepper.
- Garnish with parsley.

# Scallop and Shrimp Toss

Serves 6

1 pound fettuccine
1½ pounds sea scallops
2 Tbls. butter
1½ pounds shrimp, cooked, deveined and peeled
½ pound sugar snap peas

1 sweet red bell pepper, sliced
¼ cup olive oil
¼ cup tarragon vinegar
¼ cup fresh basil, chopped
¼ cup fresh lemon juice

- Cook fettuccine according to instructions. Drain. Cool.
- In a skillet saute the scallops for 4 minutes. Cool.
- In a salad bowl toss together all the ingredients.
- Freshly grated parmesan cheese can be served with the toss.

# Seafood Fettuccine

Serves 6

1 pound shrimp, cooked, peeled and deveined

1 pound smoked scallops

1 pound smoked salmon, broken into small pieces

1 pound fettuccine

- ◆ Cook fettuccine according to instructions. Drain. Place in serving bowl.
- ◆ Toss with seafood and Cream Sauce.

*Cream Sauce*

1 stick butter

½ cup flour

1½ cups half and half

½ cup dry white wine

½ cup grated parmesan cheese

Salt and pepper

- ◆ In a sauce pan melt the butter. Stir in the flour and slowly add the half and half until thickened. Stir in the wine, cheese, salt and pepper.

# Angel Hair Pasta with Lobster

Serves 6

1 pound angel hair pasta

2 pounds lobster meat

- ◆ Cook the pasta according to directions. Drain. Place in serving bowl.
- ◆ Toss with lobster and champagne basil sauce.

*Champagne Basil Sauce*

2 Tbls. butter

2 shallots, finely chopped

4 button mushrooms, chopped

¼ cup flour

½ cup Champagne

Pinch of saffron

¼ cup basil, finely chopped

1 cup heavy cream

- ◆ Melt the butter in a sauce pan and saute mushrooms and shallots. Add flour and stir in cream until thickened.
- ◆ Stir in champagne, saffron and basil.

# Pasta with Lobster

Serves 6

1 pound shrimp, cooked, deveined and peeled
2 pounds lobster meat

1 pound angel hair pasta
Grated parmesan cheese

- Cook pasta according to instructions. Drain. Place in serving bowl.
- Toss with lobster, shrimp. Add Garlic and Butter Sauce.
- Sprinkle with parmesan cheese.

*Garlic and Butter Sauce*

1 stick butter
½ cup flour
1 cup heavy cream
1 cup half and half

4 garlic cloves, crushed
1 shallot, peeled and chopped
Salt and Pepper

- In a sauce pan melt the butter and saute the garlic and shallot. Stir in the flour. Slowly add the cream and half and half until thickened.
- Season with salt and pepper.

# Lobster with Penne

Serves 6

1 pound penne
2 pounds lobster meat
1 pound asparagus, cut into 1 inch pieces
1 cup fresh corn

2 leeks, sliced
2 Tbls. butter
Garlic Sauce (see recipe above)
Freshly grated parmesan cheese

- Cook the penne according to directions. Drain.
- In a skillet melt the butter and cook the asparagus, corn and leeks for 3 minutes. Add the lobster.
- In a serving bowl toss the penne, lobster, vegetables and Garlic Sauce.
- Sprinkle with grated parmesan cheese.

# Dilled Scallops

Serves 4

1½ pounds scallops
¼ cup olive oil
Juice of 1 lemon
Salt and pepper
½ pound button mushrooms, sliced
2 cloves garlic, chopped

¼ cup flour
1 cup chicken stock
½ cup dry white wine
½ cup whipping cream
2 Tbls. fresh dill, snipped
½ pound fettuccine, cooked
Freshly grated parmesan cheese

- In a bowl toss together the scallops, 2 Tbls. olive oil, lemon juice, salt and pepper. Cover and chill for 30 minutes.
- In a skillet saute the mushrooms in the remaining olive oil.
- Add scallops for 3-4 minutes. Remove scallops and mushrooms from skillet.
- In the skillet saute the garlic and whisk in the flour.
- Stir in the chicken broth and white wine.
- Stir in cream until thickened. Add dill.
- Place the fettuccine in a large serving bowl or on individual plates.
- Spoon scallops and mushrooms over the fettuccine. Top with the cream sauce.
- Sprinkle parmesan cheese over the sauce.

# Fettuccine with Smoked Chicken

Serves 6

1 pound fettuccine
2 pounds smoked chicken, cut into bitesize pieces

3 large tomatoes, chopped
¼ cup fresh basil, chopped

- Cook the fettuccine according to directions. Drain.
- In a serving dish toss the fettuccine, chicken, tomatoes and basil with the sauce.

*Cream Sauce with Parmesan Cheese and Pine Nuts*

1 stick butter
½ cup flour
2 cups half and half

1 cup parmesan cheese
½ cup pine nuts
Salt and pepper

- Melt the butter in a sauce pan and stir in flour.
- Slowly add half and half until thickened. Stir in parmesan cheese, pine nuts, salt and pepper.

# Smoked Chicken with Penne

Serves 6

1 pound penne
6 boneless smoked chicken breasts
½ pound sundried tomatoes

4½ ounce can artichoke hearts, quartered
½ pound fresh Mozzarella

- Cook the penne according to the directions. Drain.
- Put the penne in a casserole, layer with chicken breasts, artichoke hearts, sundried tomatoes and then mozzarella.
- Put under the broiler until cheese bubbles. Serve immediately.

# Mediterranean Chicken Fettuccine

Serves 6

6 boneless chicken breasts
14½ ounce can artichoke hearts, quartered
1 large can black olives

6 Roma tomatoes, sliced
2 green onions, chopped
½ cup fresh basil, chopped
1 lb. spinach fettuccine, cooked

♦ Grill chicken on BBQ.
♦ On each plate divide up the fettucine, top with a chicken breast, and then other ingredients Spoon the Ouzo Cream Sauce over top.

*Ouzo Cream Sauce*

1 stick butter
½ cup flour

2 cups cream
½ cup Ouzo

♦ Melt the butter in a sauce pan and stir flour, then add cream and Ouzo. Stir until thickened.

# Fettuccine Carbonara

Serves 6

1 pound fettuccine
½ stick butter
1 cup cream
4 cloves garlic, crushed
1 pound fresh peas

12 slices bacon, cooked and crumbled
¼ cup fresh parsley
Freshly grated parmesan cheese.

♦ Cook the fettuccine according to instructions. Drain and remove from pot.
♦ Melt the butter in the pot and saute the garlic and fresh peas. Add the cream and parsley. Stir in the fettuccine and bacon.
♦ Serve hot with grated parmesan cheese.

# Pasta with Spinach Sauce

Serves 6 as a side dish

1 pound penne

Cook penne according to instructions and drain. Place in covered serving bowl.

*Spinach Sauce*

2 Tbls. olive oil
2 Tbls. butter
¼ cup onion, chopped
2 cloves garlic, chopped
¼ cup white wine

1 cup heavy cream
1 cup chicken stock
½ pound fresh spinach
¼ cup fresh basil, chopped

- Heat the oil and butter in a sauce pan, and add the onions, then garlic.
- Add wine and reduce by half.
- Add cream and stock and reduce by half again.
- Add spinach and basil until wilted.
- Serve over penne.

# Asparagus and Pasta

Serves 4

1 pound young thin asparagus, sliced in 1 inch pieces
½ pound tagliatelle
2 Tbls. butter
1 cup heavy cream
Salt and pepper

1 Tbls. flat leaf parsley
1 Tbls. snipped chives
1 Tbls. fresh dill
1 Tbls. chopped rosemary
Fresh grated parmesan cheese

- Cook the tagliatelle according to directions. Drain. Place in covered serving bowl.
- In a sauce pan melt the butter and cook the asparagus for 3 minutes.
- Stir in all the ingredients, except cheese.
- Sprinkle cheese on top.

# Green Noodles

Serves 6

1 pound spinach noodles
½ stick butter, melted
¼ cup fresh basil
1 teaspoon oregano

½ teaspoon fresh ground pepper
½ teaspoon coarse salt
½ cup fresh grated parmesan cheese.

- ◆ Cook noodles according to directions. Drain and put into a serving dish.
- ◆ Stir in butter and then other ingredients.
- ◆ Serve immediately with veal or lamb.


# Pasta Primavera

Serves 4

2 Tbls. olive oil
½ pound spinach fettuccine
1 pound fresh peas
1 cup broccoli head
1 leek, chopped

½ pound asparagus, cut in 1" slices
Parmesan cheese

- ◆ Cook the fettuccine according to instructions. Drain.
- ◆ In a skillet heat the oil and quickly cook the vegetables for 3 minutes.
- ◆ Combine the fettuccine and vegetables in a serving dish.
- ◆ Toss with herb cream sauce and sprinkle parmesan cheese on top.

*Herb Cream Sauce*

½ stick butter
¼ cup flour
1 cup half and half
½ cup Chardonnay
2 Tbls. fresh basil, chopped

2 Tbls. fresh parsley, chopped
½ teaspoon thyme
½ teaspoon sage
Salt and pepper

- ◆ In a sauce pan melt the butter. Add the flour and stir in cream until thickened. Add Chardonnay and herbs.

# Vegetable Linguine with Garlic Sauce

Serves 6-8

1 pound linguine
½ stick unsalted butter
1 large zucchini, sliced thinly
1 yellow squash, sliced thinly

1 pound green beans, trimmed
½ pound sundried tomatoes
¼ cup fresh basil

- Cook linguine according to directions. Drain and place in serving dish with a top.
- In a skillet melt the butter and saute the zucchini, squash and beans until tender. Stir in the tomatoes and basil.
- Spoon over the linguine. Add Garlic Sauce.

*Garlic Sauce with White Wine*

1 stick butter
½ cup flour
1 cup heavy cream

1 cup half and half
½ cup white wine
4 cloves garlic, crushed

- In a sauce pan melt the butter and saute the garlic. Stir in the flour and slowly add the half and half and cream. Stir in the white wine.
- Serve over the linguine. This can be topped with grated parmesan cheese.

# Pesto Vegetable Pasta

Serves 4 as a side dish

½ pound fettuccine
2 Tbls. butter
½ pound green beans, trimmed
1 medium zucchini, sliced

1 red bell pepper, sliced
Pesto
Fresh grated parmesan cheese

- Cook fettuccine according to directions. Drain and put in a covered serving dish.
- In a skillet melt the butter and saute the green beans, zucchini and pepper until tender. Add the pesto.
- Spoon over the fettuccine. Top with freshly grated parmesan cheese.

# Linguine with Parmesan Cream Sauce

Serves 6-8

1 pound linguine
½ stick butter
1 lb. button mushrooms, sliced

2 Tbls shallots, chopped
2 cloves garlic, minced

- Cook linguine according to instructions. Drain and place in a serving dish.
- Melt the butter in a skillet and saute the mushrooms, shallots and garlic. Stir into linguine. Add sauce.

*Parmesan Cream Sauce*

1 stick butter
2 cups half and half
½ cup flour

¼ cup Sherry
1 cup freshly grated parmesan cheese

- Melt the butter in a saucepan. Add the flour and slowly stir in the half and half. As it thickens stir in the Sherry.
- Pour over the linguine and serve with grated parmesan cheese.

# Lobster Risotto

Serves 4

2 Tbls. butter
1 small onion, chopped
2 cloves garlic, chopped
1½ cups arborio rice
½ cup dry white wine
4 cups chicken stock
1 cup fresh snap peas

½ teaspoon salt
½ teaspoon pepper
¼ cup fresh basil
1½ pounds fresh lobster meat
Fresh parmesan cheese

- In a sauce pan melt the butter and add the onion. Stir in the rice and slowly add the stock and white wine. Stir until liquid is absorbed and rice is tender. Stir in the snap peas, salt, pepper and basil.
- Gently fold in the lobster. Top with grated parmesan cheese. Serve hot.

# Mussel Risotto

Serves 4

2 Tbls. butter
1 small onion, chopped
1 cup arborio rice
½ cup white wine
3 cups fish stock

4 dozen mussels
¼ cup fresh parsley, chopped
Juice 1 lemon
Salt and pepper
Freshly grated parmesan cheese

- In a sauce pan melt the butter and add the onion. Stir in the rice and slowly stir in the rice until all the liquid is absorbed, and rice is tender.
- Wash and clean the beards off the mussels. In a large pot combine the white wine and mussels. Cook until the mussels open. Discard shells.
- Add mussels and wine broth to the rice.
- Stir in salt and pepper taste, parsley and lemon juice.
- Serve hot with parmesan cheese.

# Red Pepper Couscous

Serves 6

1 box couscous
1 cup chicken stock
¼ cup onion, chopped
½ cup red pepper, chopped
½ teaspoon salt

1 Tbls fresh mint, chopped
2 Tbls. cilantro, chopped
Pepper
1 orange, thinly sliced
1 lemon, thinly sliced

- Cook couscous according to directions on package, but substitute 1 cup chicken stock for water.
- In a bowl combine all ingredients except lemon and orange slices. Add couscous.
- Place couscous in a serving bowl.
- Garnish with orange and lemon slices.
- Serve hot or chilled.
- 3 cups cooked rice can be substituted for the couscous.

# Fall Couscous

Serves 8

6 cups chicken stock
3 cups couscous
2 Tbls. orange rind, grated
½ cup green onions, finely
chopped

1 cup cranberries
Salt and pepper

- Place the broth in a saucepan and bring to a boil.
- Stir in the couscous and simmer for 5 minutes. Remove from heat. Stir in the remaining ingredients.
- For a spicier couscous, add ¼ teaspoon cayenne.

# Couscous Cakes

These are very good served with lamb.

Serves 4

1 cup couscous
2 cups water
2 Tbls. butter
1 teaspoon salt
1 small onion, chopped

2 Tbls. vegetable oil
2 eggs
½ cup parsley
½ cup mint
Vegetable oil for frying

- Combine the water, butter and salt in a sauce pan and bring to a boil. Stir in the couscous. Turn off heat and let sit 5 minutes.
- In a skillet heat 2 Tbls. vegetable oil and add onion, until just translucent.
- In a large bowl beat the eggs, add the couscous, onion, parsley and mint. Form into small cakes. Chill for 1 hour.
- Heat oil in skillet and fry the couscous cakes until golden on each side.
- Garnish with fresh mint leaves.

# Wild Rice

Serves 4-6

1 stick butter
½ pound mushrooms, sliced
1 small onion, chopped
1 cup wild rice
¼ cup green pepper, chopped

2 cloves garlic, minced
1 cup slivered almonds
3 cups chicken stock
Salt and pepper

- Preheat oven to 350°.
- In a skillet melt the butter. Add the mushrooms, onion, green pepper and garlic. Cook for 5 minutes.
- Add almonds, rice, chicken stock, salt and pepper.
- Turn into a buttered 1½ quart casserole and bake 1hour.


# Rice with Apricots

Serves 12

2 cups dried apricots
1 cup raisins or currants
1 cup water
1 cup onion, chopped

½ cup green pepper, chopped
½ cup butter
Salt and pepper
6 cups cooked rice

- Preheat oven to 375°.
- Soak the apricots and raisins in water for ½ hour. Drain and chop finely.
- In a large pan saute the onion and pepper in the butter. Add the rice, raisins and apricots. Add salt and pepper to taste.
- Pour mixture into a large buttered casserole.
- Bake for 40 minutes. Serve hot or chilled.

# Rice with Cranberries

Serves 8

2 cups fresh cranberries
½ cup sugar
1 medium onion, chopped

2 cups rice
6 cups chicken stock

- Preheat oven to 350°.
- Combine all the ingredients in a 1½ quart casserole.
- Cover and bake for 45 minutes, or until all the stock is absorbed.

# Tabbouleh

Tabbouleh is so refreshing on a hot summer day. Serve with lamb kabobs or grilled lamb.

Serves 6

1 cup burghal (crushed wheat)
3 large tomatoes, chopped
1 cup parsley, finely chopped
1 cup onions, chopped

¼ cup fresh lemon juice
¼ cup olive oil
¼ cup fresh mint, chopped

- Place the burghal in a bowl and cover with cold water. Let sit for 10 minutes. Then drain in a colander.
- In a bowl combine all the ingredients.
- Serve chilled or at room temperature.

# Breads, Biscuits, and Coffee Cakes

**Old Mill**

The Old Mill on Prospect Street was built c1746. The mill is still in operation and daily grinds corn.

Tuckernuck Island, just off Nantucket, is an Indian word meaning "Loaf of Bread". The island was originally connected to Nantucket and farmed. Today a few houses remain.

On July 10, 1883 Nathan Chapman was granted a patent for a bread cutter, patent 280,796. He owned the Veranda House, later The Overlook.

The Nantucket Bake Shop has been an Island favorite for half a century. Aime Poirie was the first baker to sell Portuguese bread. She owned the shop during the 1960s and 70s. In 1965 the bakery was sold to Joe Cecot, and to Anne and David Bradt in 1976.

# Cranberry Scones

Makes about 8-10 scones.

2 cups flour
2 teaspoons baking powder
½ teaspoon salt
½ stick unsalted butter
2 eggs

½ cup heavy cream
2 Tbls. sugar
1 cup cranberries
2 Tbls. orange rind

- Preheat oven to 425°.
- Combine the flour, baking powder, sugar, and salt in a large mixing bowl.
- Using a pastry blender, work in the butter until it is similar to coarse meal.
- Add the eggs one at a time, and then the cream, cranberries and orange rind.
- Turn the dough out onto a lightly floured board, and knead until smooth, about 2 minutes.
- Roll out the dough until about ¾" thick. Cut out the scones with a 3" cookie cutter.
- Place on an ungreased baking sheet. Cook for 15-20 minutes, or until golden.
- Serve with whipped cream, crème fraiche, cream cheese or butter.

# Cranberry Buns

1 cup milk
4 cups flour
¼ cup sugar
1 teaspoon salt
1 teaspoon lemon peel, grated

2 sticks butter, softened
1 pkg. yeast
¼ cup warm water
2 eggs, beaten

- In a sauce pan scald the milk. Cool to lukewarm.
- In a large bowl combine the flour sugar, salt and lemon peel. Cut in the butter.
- Dissolve the yeast in the warm water. Add to flour mixture. Then add milk and eggs. Cover dough tightly and let rise for at least 2 hours.
- Divide dough in half. On a floured board, roll out the dough into a 8" x 15" rectangle.
- Spread filling on dough. Fold dough into a 3 layer strip 15" long. Cut dough into 13 strips. Hold ends of each strip and twist lightly in opposite directions. Pinch the ends to seal. Place on a greased baking sheet.
- Bake in oven 10-15 minutes. Cool on wire racks.
- Frost with confectioner's sugar frosting.

*Filling*

1½ cups cranberries
½ cup sugar
½ cup raisins

½ cup pecans
¼ cup honey
2 Tbls. orange peel, grated

- In a sauce pan combine all the ingredients and bring to a boil. Cook for five minutes. Cool.

*Confectioner's Sugar Frosting*

2 cups confectioner's sugar
½ cup milk

½ stick butter
1 teaspoon vanilla

- In a bowl beat together all ingredients until just slightly runny.
- Spread on top of each bun after baking. Garnish with a cranberry.

# Cranberry Bread

1¼ cups cranberries, cut in half
1 cup sugar
Juice of 1 large orange
Rind of 1 orange, grated
1 egg, beaten
½ stick butter, melted

2 cups flour
1 teaspoon baking powder
½ teaspoon baking soda
½ teaspoon salt
½ cup walnuts or pecans

- ◆ In a bowl combine the cranberries, sugar, orange juice and orange rind. Refrigerate overnight.
- ◆ Next day add the other ingredients. Pour into a loaf pan.
- ◆ Bake at 350° for one hour.
- ◆ For a spicier loaf add 1 teaspoon cinnamon, ¼ teaspoon ginger and ¼ teaspoon nutmeg or allspice.
- ◆ Muffins, rather than bread, can be made using the same recipe and muffin tins.

*Aunt Edith Stonestreet's Recipe*

# Apricot Bread

2 cups flour
3 teaspoons baking powder
¼ teaspoon baking soda
½ teaspoon salt
1 egg, beaten
1 cup sugar

2 Tbls. butter, melted
¾ cup orange juice
1 cup pecans or walnuts
¾ cup dried apricots, chopped

- ◆ Preheat oven to 350°.
- ◆ In a bowl combine the flour, baking powder, baking soda and salt. Add egg, sugar, butter, orange juice and nuts. Fold in apricots.
- ◆ Bake for 1 ¼ hours in loaf pan.
- ◆ Serve with cream cheese.

*Mrs. M. B. Morgan's (formerly of Martin's Lane) Recipe*

# Portuguese Bread

2 cups boiling water
3 Tbls. sugar
3 teaspoons salt

3 packages yeast
6 cups flour

♦ Combine the first 3 ingredients. Cool to lukewarm. Add yeast. Stir in the flour.
♦ Knead the dough. Grease a bowl with olive oil. Place the dough and let rise (about 1 hour), or until doubled in size.
♦ Punch down the dough and divide into 2 loaves. Place on an oiled cookie sheet. Let rise again (about 1 hour).
♦ Bake at 400° until golden.

# Spoon Bread

1½ cups cornmeal
1 teaspoon sugar
1 teaspoon salt
1½ cups boiling water

½ stick butter, melted
5 eggs
2 cups milk
1 Tbls. baking powder

♦ Preheat the oven to 350°.
♦ Combine the cornmeal, sugar and salt. Scald with the boiling water. Add the melted butter.
♦ Beat the eggs in a separate bowl, and add the milk.
♦ Combine the two mixtures. Add the baking powder.
♦ Pour into a greased 9" x 13" glass baking dish.
♦ Bake 30-40 minutes until browned.

# Corn Bread

2 eggs
1 cup sour cream
1 cup milk
½ stick butter
2 cups yellow cornmeal

2 cups flour
2 teaspoons baking powder
1 Tbls. sugar
1 teaspoon salt
1 cup fresh corn

- Preheat the oven to 425°.
- Grease a large iron skillet and heat in oven.
- Beat together the eggs, sour cream, milk and butter in a bowl.
- Add the dry ingredients and corn. Pour into heated skillet.
- Bake until browned about 20-25 minutes.
- For a spicier bread add 2 Tbls. chopped jalapeno chilies.
- 1 cup grated cheddar cheese is also good.

# Pumpkin Bread

1½ cups sugar
½ stick butter
2 cups flour
¼ teaspoon baking powder
1 teaspoon baking soda
½ teaspoon salt
1 cup pumpkin puree

1 teaspoon nutmeg
1 teaspoon allspice
1 teaspoon cinnamon
½ teaspoon ground cloves
2 eggs
½ cup pecans or walnuts

- Preheat oven to 350°.
- Beat the butter and sugar together. Add the other ingredients.
- Pour into a greased loaf pan.
- Bake 30 minutes, or until a toothpick comes out dry.
- Serve with cream cheese.

# Pumpkin Seed Bread

Makes 2 loaves

2 teaspoons yeast
1 teaspoon sugar
½ cup warm milk
1 cup warm water
3 cups flour
2 Tbls sesame seeds

1 cup cornmeal
2 teaspoons salt
2 Tbls. pumpkin seeds
2 Tbls. sunflower seeds

- ♦ In a bowl combine the yeast, sugar, milk and water. Let sit for 10 minutes.
- ♦ In another bowl combine the flour, cornmeal and salt. Add to the yeast.
- ♦ On a floured board knead the dough for 5 minutes. Add the seeds. Knead for 5 minutes.
- ♦ Divide the dough into two and shape each into a circle about 6" in diameter. Place each in a loaf pan. Cover with a damp cloth and let rise 1 hour, or until double in size.
- ♦ Preheat oven to 400°.
- ♦ Bake bread for 10 minutes and then reduce heat to 300°. Cook for 25 minutes or until golden brown.

# Drop Donut Balls

½ cup sugar
½ cup milk
1 egg
2 Tbls. cooking oil
1 ½ cups flour

2 Tbls. baking powder
½ teaspoon cinnamon
½ teaspoon salt
½ teaspoon nutmeg
Oil

- ♦ Combine all the ingredients in a bowl.
- ♦ In a skillet or electric frying pan heat the oil until bubbly.
- ♦ Drop by teaspoons into the oil, and cook until just browned.
- ♦ Roll in sugar, mixture of sugar and cinnamon, or maple syrup.

# Blueberry Coffee Cake/Muffins

1 stick butter, softened
1 cup sugar
2 eggs
1 cup sour cream

1½ teaspoons baking powder
1½ cups flour
1 teaspoon vanilla
2 cups blueberries

- Cream the butter and sugar in a bowl. Beat in the eggs and sour cream. Add flour, baking powder, and vanilla. Gently fold in the blueberries.
- Pour into a buttered 9' baking dish or muffin tins. Spoon on topping.

*Topping*

¼ cup sugar
¼ cup brown sugar

2 teaspoons cinnamon
½ cup walnuts or pecans

- Preheat oven to 350°
- Combine the ingredients and spoon over the batter.
- Bake about 45 minutes, or until a toothpick comes out dry from the batter.
- 1 cup sliced fresh peaches can be added or used in place of the blueberries.

# Apple Cheddar Biscuits

Makes 6-8 biscuits

6 Tbls. butter, softened
2 cups flour
¾ cup half and half
2 teaspoons baking powder
2 Tbls. sugar

½ cup sharp cheddar cheese
1 large apple, peeled, cored and diced

- Preheat oven to 450°.
- In a food processor blend all the ingredients, except the apple.
- Stir in the apple until just crunchy.
- Drop by large spoonfuls onto an ungreased baking sheet.
- Bake 10 minutes or until just browned.

# Chocolate Nut Coffee Cake

*Batter*

1 cup sugar
2 sticks unsalted butter, softened
3 eggs

1 cup sour cream
2 ½ cups flour
½ teaspoon baking soda

- ◆ Preheat oven to 325°.
- ◆ In a bowl cream the sugar and butter. Add the eggs, sour cream, flour and baking soda.
- ◆ Pour ½ of the batter into a 8" square baking dish. Add ½ of topping. Repeat.
- ◆ Bake 50 minutes.

*Topping*

1 cup walnuts or pecans
½ cup sugar

1 cup chocolate morsels

- ◆ In a bowl combine the ingredients
- ◆ Butterscotch or peanut butter morsels can be substituted for the chocolate morsels.

# Strawberry Bread

1 stick butter
½ cup sugar
1 egg
1 ½ cups flour
½ teaspoon salt

½ teaspoon baking soda
½ teaspoon cinnamon
1 pint strawberries, washed, stems removed, and sliced
½ cup pecans

- ◆ Preheat oven to 350°.
- ◆ In a bowl cream butter and sugar.
- ◆ Add egg, then dry ingredients.
- ◆ Fold in strawberries and pecans.
- ◆ Bake 50-60 minutes, or until a toothpick comes out dry.
- ◆ Serve toasted with cream cheese.

# Egg and Brunch Dishes

**Old North Wharf**

**Sunday Brunch**

*Bloody Mary*
*Kir*
*Lobster Benedict*
*Baked Tomatoes*
*Sweet Rolls*
*Fresh Fruit*

# Lobster Benedict

Serves 4

4 English muffins, halved          8 eggs
1 pound lobster meat               Paprika

♦ Toast the English muffins.
♦ Either poach or hard boil the eggs.
♦ Spoon the lobster meat on the muffins and place an egg on each muffin.
♦ Top with Hollandaise sauce. Sprinkle with paprika.

*Hollandaise Sauce*

3 egg yolks                        Juice of 1 lemon
2 sticks butter

♦ Melt the butter in a sauce pan.
♦ Put the yolks and lemon juice in a food processor. Slowly add the butter until thickened.

# Creamed Lobster

Serves 4

½ stick butter
½ cup flour
2 cups half and half
½ cup dry Sherry

8 hard boiled eggs, sliced
4 toasted English muffins or 2 cups cooked rice
1 pound lobster meat

- In a sauce pan melt the butter. Stir in the flour, and then half and half until thickened. Add Sherry.
- On each half muffin arrange the egg slices, then lobster. Spoon the sauce over the lobster.
- Serve immediately.

# Spinach and Mushroom Crepes

Makes 8 crepes

1 egg
1 cup milk

1 teaspoon baking powder
1 cup flour

- Combine the ingredients in a bowl.
- In a crepe pan or small skillet with melted butter cook 8 thin pancakes. Set aside.

½ stick butter
1 large onion, chopped
1 pound mushrooms, sliced
¼ cup chopped parsley

1 pound fresh spinach, stems removed
Hollandaise Sauce

- Melt the butter in a skillet and saute onions and mushrooms.
- Add the parsley and spinach until just wilted. Spread over the crepes.
- Roll the crepes.
- Pour the Hollandaise sauce over the crepes.
- Serve immediately, or place in oven to just warm.
- 2 cups cooked scallops, lobster meat, chicken or ham can be added to the filling.

173

# Spinach Omelette

Serves 2

4 eggs, separated
1 cup fresh baby spinach leaves
1 small tomato, chopped
4 slices bacon, cooked

½ cup Gruyere or Swiss cheese
¼ cup fresh basil chopped
Salt and pepper
2 Tbls. butter

- ◆ Preheat oven to 350°.
- ◆ In a bowl beat the egg whites until stiff.
- ◆ In another bowl beat the egg yolks, salt and pepper. Fold in the egg whites.
- ◆ Melt the butter in an iron skillet and quickly wilt the spinach. Remove and add more butter to the skillet. Add the eggs, scraping sides to keep from sticking. Cook for 4 minutes, or until the eggs just begin to set.
- ◆ Add the other ingredients. Fold the omelet in half. Place in the oven and let set, no more than 10 minutes.
- ◆ The omelet can also be put under the broiler until just set.
- ◆ Garnish with fresh basil and tomato slices.

# Crab Frittata

Serves 4

2 Tbls. butter
8 eggs, separated
3 Tbls. butter
1 pound crab meat

1 cup grated cheddar cheese
¼ cup fresh parsley
Salt and pepper

- ◆ Preheat oven to 350°.
- ◆ In a bowl beat the egg whites until stiff.
- ◆ In another bowl beat the egg yolks salt and pepper. Fold in the egg whites.
- ◆ Melt the butter in an iron skillet. Add the eggs, scraping sides to keep from sticking. Add the other ingredients.
- ◆ Place in the oven and bake for 20 minutes, or until set.

# Summer Omelet

Serves 2

2 Tbls. butter
4 eggs
1 small tomato, finely chopped
2 Tbls. chives

1 Tbls. fresh basil, chopped
2 Tbls. red pepper, chopped
Salt and pepper to taste

- In a bowl beat the eggs.
- Melt the butter in a skillet. Pour eggs into the skillet, scrapping sides to keep from sticking.
- Add tomato, chives, basil and salt and pepper.
- When the eggs are set, carefully fold the omelet in half. Place on cutting board. Cut in half.
- Serve on individual plates garnished with fresh basil leaves.

# Bacon and Cheese Frittata

Serves 2

4 eggs
4 slices bacon
¼ cup onion, chopped

½ cup cheddar cheese, grated
4 black pitted olives, sliced
Salt and pepper

- Cook the bacon in a skillet until crisp. Remove from skillet, drain and crumble.
- Cook the onion in the bacon fat. Remove onion and drain fat.
- Combine the bacon, onion and sliced olives in a bowl.
- In another bowl beat the eggs. Add bacon mixture.
- Heat the skillet with the remaining bacon fat (a small amount of butter might need to be added).
- Pour the egg mixture into the skillet, and scrape sides to prevent sticking. Do not stir, but let sit until eggs are set.
- This also can be cooked in a 350° oven for about 15 minutes, or until the eggs are set.

# Sausage and Tomato Quiche

*Pastry*

1¼ cups flour
1 stick butter

¼ cup water
3 ounces cream cheese

- Combine all ingredients in food processor until a ball forms.
- On a floured board roll into the shape of 9" deep dish pie pan and place in pie pan.

*Filling*

3 medium tomatoes, sliced
1 pound sausage
¼ cup chives, chopped
3 eggs, separated

1 cup Swiss cheese, grated
¾ cup sour cream
½ cup flour
Salt and pepper, to taste

- Preheat oven to 350°.
- Brown the sausage and chives in a skillet. Pour into pie crust. Place tomato slices on top.
- In a bowl beat the egg whites until stiff.
- In a separate bowl combine the yolks with the sour cream. Add the flour, salt and pepper. Beat until smooth.
- Fold in the egg whites. Pour over the cheese.
- Bake for 25 minutes or until golden brown.

# Granola

3 cups whole wheat flour
2 cups corn meal
1 cup wheat germ
3 cups coconut
6 cups oatmeal

1 cup honey
1 cup vegetable oil
1-2 cups water
1 cup nuts, raisins, or sunflower seeds

- Combine the dry ingredients. Add the other ingredients. Combine until crumbly.
- Bake in slow oven 250° stirring every 15 minutes until dry and light brown. Store in dry container.

# Quahaug Pie

Serves 4-6

9" pie crust
2 dozen quahaugs
½ cup onion, chopped
2 cups potatoes, cubed
¼ cup butter

¼ cup flour
¾ cup light cream
¼ teaspoon thyme
1 teaspoon pepper
1 teaspoon salt

- Preheat oven to 400°.
- Place the clams on a baking sheet and put in oven until clam shells open. Remove clams from shells and reserve liquor. Grind up the clams with the liquor.
- In a covered sauce pan boil the potatoes and onions in water until tender. Drain.
- In the sauce pan combine the clams, cubed potatoes, onion, thyme, salt, and pepper. Bring to a boil.
- Stir in the butter and add the flour, then cream, until thickened.
- Butter a casserole and pour in the clam mixture.
- Top with pie crust. Prick the crust with a fork.
- Bake 30 minutes or until pastry is golden brown.

# Apple Pancakes

- Makes about 8 small pancakes.

1 cup flour
¼ teaspoon salt
¼ cup sugar
1 tablespoon baking powder
1 egg
1 cup milk

¼ cup sour cream
½ teaspoon cinnamon
1 cup apples, peeled, cored, and diced
2 tablespoons melted butter

- In a bowl beat egg, milk and sour cream. Add salt, sugar, baking powder, flour, cinnamon, then butter. Stir in the apples.
- Pour the batter by large spoonsful into a skillet and cook about 4 minutes to a side.
- Serve with butter, maple syrup and sausage.

# Blueberry Pancakes

Serves 2-3

| | |
|---|---|
| 1 cup flour | 1 egg |
| ¼ teaspoon salt | 1 cup milk |
| 2 Tbls. sugar | ¼ cup sour cream |
| 1 Tbls. baking powder | 2 Tbls. butter, melted |
| | 1 cup blueberries |

- In a bowl beat the egg, milk and sour cream.
- Add the other ingredients except the blueberries and butter. Dredge the blueberries in small amount of flour to keep from bleeding. With a spoon gently stir in the blueberries.
- In a skillet or griddle melt the butter. Add to batter.
- Drop batter by large spoonfuls onto griddle. Cook pancakes on each side until golden brown.
- Serve with butter, maple syrup, or honey.

# Blueberry Waffles

Makes six waffles

| | |
|---|---|
| 3 eggs | ¼ cup sugar |
| 1½ cups milk | 4 tablespoons melted butter |
| 1¾ cups flour | 1 pint blueberries |
| 2 teaspoons baking powder | 1 cup heavy cream, whipped |

- Separate the eggs. Beat together the yolks and milk. Add the dry ingredients and butter.
- Beat the egg whites until stiff. Fold the egg whites in with the other ingredients.
- Heat the waffle iron.
- Pour the batter by large spoonsful into the waffle iron. Be careful not to get too close to the side. Cook until browned.
- Serve the waffles with blueberries and whipped cream.
- Syrup or honey can be substituted for the whipped cream.
- Strawberries can be substituted for the blueberries.

# Codfish Cakes

Serves 4-6

1 pound salted codfish
1 medium onion, chopped

6 slices bacon
4 cups mashed potatoes

- ◆ Soak the codfish overnight in water, refrigerated.
- ◆ Boil the codfish in a saucepan, and the drain at least twice. Place the codfish in a mixing bowl and break up. Add the mashed potatoes.
- ◆ In a skillet brown the bacon. Remove the bacon and add the onion and saute until just browned. Add to the codfish.
- ◆ Shape into cakes. Melt the butter in a skillet and saute until browned on each side.
- ◆ Serve on a platter garnished with parsley. Ketchup should be served with the codfish cakes.
- ◆ Grilled salmon can be substituted for the codfish.

# Fish Hash

Serves 4

2 cups cold cooked fish (tuna, salmon, cod, your choice)
½ cup onions, chopped
2 cups potatoes, peeled and diced

¼ cup butter
Salt and pepper
1 teaspoon fresh rosemary
½ teaspoon cayenne

- ◆ In a skillet melt the butter and saute the onions and potatoes until tender.
- ◆ Add the fish, salt, pepper, rosemary and cayenne. Cook over high heat until the hash begins to brown and get crispy.
- ◆ Serve immediately with ketchup or tomato salsa.
- ◆ This can also be baked in the oven until browned.

# Creamed Finnan Haddie

Finnan haddie is smoked haddock.

Serves 4

½ cup butter
½ cup flour
2 cups half and half

2 pounds finnan haddie, broken up into small pieces
4 English muffins or 2 cups cooked rice

- In a saucepan melt the butter. Stir in the flour and slowly add the half and half until thickened.
- Add finnan haddie.
- Serve on toasted English muffins, or rice.
- Dried codfish can be substituted for the finnan haddie.

# Smoked Salmon Crepes

Serves 4

½ pound smoked salmon
1 large cucumber, peeled and thinly sliced
1 small jar red caviar

Crepes (p
½ cup sour cream
1 Tbls. lime juice
¼ cup fresh dill

- In a bowl combine the caviar, sour cream, lime juice and dill. Spread on each crepe.
- Place a slice of salmon on top and roll up.
- Serve immediately.
- This also is good as an appetizer.

# *Sandwiches*

**The author and her daughter – Dionis beach picnic**

# Scallop Caesar Wrap

Serves 4

4 tortillas
1 pound scallops
 Romaine lettuce
2 garlic cloves, halved
¼ cup olive oil

Juice of 1 lemon
¼ cup freshly grated parmesan cheese
Salt and pepper

♦ Rub the garlic around the sides of a salad bowl. Add salt, pepper, lemon juice and olive oil.
♦ Tear the lettuce into bite size pieces and add to the bowl. Stir in the parmesan cheese.
♦ Grill the scallops.
♦ Lay out the tortillas and spread with romaine salad and scallops. Roll up and cut in half.
♦ Sliced tomatoes also can be added to the wrap.
♦ Swordfish or lobster meat can be substituted for the scallops.


# Swordfish Tacos

Serves 4

1½ pounds swordfish
1½ cups salsa
1 can black olives, sliced
Lettuce
2 large tomatoes, diced

1 cup Monterey jack cheese with green chilies, shredded
Sour Cream
8 taco shells or tortillas

♦ Grill the swordfish. Cut into small pieces and place in taco shells or tortillas. Top with other ingredients.
♦ Salmon, cod, tuna or other seafood can be substituted for the swordfish.

# Lobster Sandwiches

Serves 4

| | |
|---|---|
| 1 pound lobster meat | Juice of ½ lemon |
| ¾ cup mayonnaise | Lettuce |
| 1 bunch watercress, chopped | Portuguese rolls, sliced |

- ◆ In a bowl combine the mayonnaise, watercress and lemon juice.
- ◆ Fold in the lobster.
- ◆ Spread the lobster mixture on the rolls with lettuce.

# Crab Sandwich

Serves 4

| | |
|---|---|
| 1 pound fresh crab meat | 1 scallion, sliced |
| 2 avocados, peeled, pitted and sliced | Juice of 1 lemon |
| | Lettuce |
| 1 cup cheddar cheese, sliced | 2 tomatoes, sliced |
| ½ cup mayonnaise | 4 English muffins |

- ◆ Preheat broiler.
- ◆ In a bowl combine the mayonnaise, scallion, lemon juice. Fold in the crab.
- ◆ Toast the English muffins on the cut side.
- ◆ Place tomato slice and some of the avocado slices on each muffin half.
- ◆ Top with crab meat and a slice of cheese.
- ◆ Place under the broiler until just bubbling.
- ◆ Lobster can be substituted for the crab.

# Seafood Sandwich

Serves 4

½ pound crab meat
½ pound shrimp, cooked, deveined and peeled
3 ounces cream cheese, softened

¼ cup mayonnaise
¼ cup fresh dill
1 scallion, chopped
Portuguese rolls

- ◆ In a bowl combine all the ingredients except the rolls.
- ◆ Spread the seafood mixture on the rolls.

# Chicken and Bacon Sandwiches

Serves 4

4 boneless chicken breasts, sliced
8 slices bacon, cooked and crumbled

½ pound cheddar cheese, sliced
Portuguese bread

- ◆ Grill the chicken breast to desired doneness.
- ◆ On a slice of bread spread the Pepper Parmesan Dressing.
- ◆ Top with the chicken, bacon and a slice of cheese.
- ◆ Cover with another slice of bread and slice in half.

*Pepper Parmesan Dressing*

½ cup mayonnaise
½ cup parmesan cheese

1 teaspoon fresh ground pepper

- ◆ Combine the ingredients in a bowl.

# BBQ Chicken Sandwich

Serves 4

4 boneless chicken breasts, sliced
4 large onions, sliced
¼ cup sugar

½ stick butter
½ pound cheddar cheese, melted
BBQ sauce, warmed
Sourdough rolls

- Grill the chicken breasts to desired doneness.
- In a skillet melt the butter and stir in onions. Add the sugar and simmer for 20 minutes.
- Melt the cheese carefully in a sauce pan.
- Cut the rolls in half. On each roll place some of the chicken and onions.
- Top with BBQ sauce and then cheese.

# Grilled Chicken Pita

Serves 4

4 grilled chicken breasts, sliced
Romaine lettuce leaves
2 red onions, sliced and grilled

2 tomatoes, sliced
4 pita bread

- Open the pita and spread with the Honey Mustard Sauce.
- Divide up the other ingredients and stuff the pita bread.

*Honey Mustard Sauce*

¼ cup Dijon mustard

¼ cup honey

- In a bowl combine the mustard and honey.

# Chicken Quesadillas

Serves 4 or more

½ cup sour cream
Juice of 1 lime
¼ cup cilantro, chopped
4 boneless chicken breasts, sliced

½ pound shredded sharp cheddar cheese
2 cups cooked rice
Tomato salsa (p.79)
Tortillas
Oil for frying

- Grill the chicken to desired doneness.
- In a bowl combine the sour cream, cilantro and lime juice. Spread on the tortillas.
- Top with some of the chicken, rice and cheese.
- Fold the tortillas in half and seal edges.
- Fry in hot oil in a skillet on both sides until golden brown.
- Remove and drain on a paper towel.
- Serve immediately with the salsa.


# Chicken Salad Sandwiches

Serves 4

2 cups cooked chicken, cubed
1 green pepper, chopped
Lettuce
2 medium tomatoes, sliced

2 green onions, chopped
½ cup mayonnaise
¼ cup fresh basil
8 slices bread

- In a bowl combine the green pepper, chicken, mayonnaise, green onions and basil.
- Place lettuce leaves and tomatoes on the bread.
- Top with chicken salad.

# Souffled Chicken Sandwiches

Makes 4 sandwiches

2 cups cooked chicken, diced
1 can deviled ham
¼ cup mayonnaise
½ teaspoon Worcestershire
4 eggs, separated

1 teaspoon baking powder
¼ cup mayonnaise
1 Tbls. Dijon mustard
4 English muffins
2 Tbls. butter, melted

♦ Preheat broiler.
♦ Split the English muffins and place on cookie sheet. Brush the muffins with the melted butter.
♦ Toast the split side under the broiler.
♦ In a bowl beat the egg whites until stiff.
♦ In a bowl combine the baking powder, mustard and egg yolks. Fold into egg whites.
♦ In another bowl combine the chicken, deviled ham, mayonnaise and Worcestershire sauce. Evenly divide and spread on each of the English muffins.
♦ Top with egg white mixture.
♦ Place under broiler for 2-3 minutes, until just browned.

# Chicken Pesto Sandwiches

Serves 4

4 boneless chicken breasts, sliced
Pesto (p.203)

Mayonnaise
Lettuce
8 slices herb bread

♦ Grill chicken until desired doneness.
♦ Spread 4 slices of bread with mayonnaise and pesto.
♦ Spread one slice of bread with the chicken, lettuce and other slice of bread.

# Chicken Cheese Sandwiches

Serves 4

4 grilled chicken breasts, sliced
8 slices bacon, cooked and cut in
half

½ pound smoked gouda cheese,
sliced
BBQ sauce
8 slices bread

- ◆ On each slice of bread put some of the chicken, bacon and cheese.
  Top with your favorite BBQ sauce.
- ◆ This also is good put under the broiler.

# Souffled Ham Sandwiches

Serves 4

8 slices bread
8 slices ham
8 slices Swiss or Gruyere cheese
½ teaspoon salt
8 eggs, separated

1 teaspoon baking powder
¼ cup mayonnaise
1 teaspoon Dijon mustard
Dash of Tabasco sauce

- ◆ Preheat oven to 350°.
- ◆ Toast the bread in the oven, one side only, in a baking dish
- ◆ Place a piece of ham and cheese on the untoasted side of each piece
  of bread.
- ◆ In a bowl combine the egg whites with the salt and beat until peaks
  formed.
- ◆ Combine the mayonnaise with the egg yolks, mustard, baking powder
  and Tabasco in another bowl. Fold into the egg whites.
- ◆ Evenly pour the egg mixture over each piece of bread. Bake for 15
  minutes or until browned and puffy.
- ◆ Serve immediately.

# Cranberry Sandwiches

These are very festive at Christmas time for a tea party.

Bread

8 ounces cream cheese, softened

1 cup cranberries

¼ cup sugar

- ◆ Cut the cranberries in half.
- ◆ In a bowl combine the cranberries, sugar and cream cheese.
- ◆ Cut the bread with a 3" cookie cutter into circles. Spread each with the cranberry cream cheese.
- ◆ Cranberry chutney can be substituted for the cranberries.

# Cranberry Turkey Sandwiches

Makes 4 sandwiches

8 slices Portuguese bread

1 pound smoked turkey breast

Cranberry chutney (p.192)

Mayonnaise

Lettuce

- ◆ Spread the 4 slices of bread with mayonnaise and top with the smoked turkey, cranberry sauce and lettuce. Top with other slices of bread and cut in half.

# Veggie Sandwich

Makes 8 sandwiches

1 large cucumber, peeled and thinly sliced

14 ½ oz. can artichoke hearts, quartered

1 cup shredded carrots

1 cup bean sprouts

Lettuce

2 large tomatoes, thinly sliced

1 red onion, sliced

Hummus

Sliced herb bread

- ◆ Spread the 4 slices of bread with the hummus and divide other ingredients among the sandwiches.

# Vegetarian Sandwich

Makes 4 sandwiches

2 avocados, sliced
1 cup bean sprouts
2 large tomatoes, sliced

1 cucumber, peeled and sliced
Lettuce, shredded
Sliced herb bread

- Spread the bread with the Herb Cream Cheese.
- Top with the other ingredients.

*Herbed Cream Cheese*

1 stick butter
1 clove garlic, crushed
1 teaspoon parsley

1 teaspoon dill
8 ounces cream cheese, softened

- Combine all the ingredients in a bowl.
- If there is any left over, cover and refrigerate. Serve with crackers.

# Vegetarian Pizza

Rosemary foccaccia dough rolled out in shape of pizza pan.

*Topping*

4 medium tomatoes, sliced thin
¼ cup onion, chopped
1 medium eggplant, peeled and sliced very thin
1 large zucchini, sliced thin
2 cups mozzarella cheese
1 red bell pepper, sliced

1 green pepper, sliced
3 garlic cloves, crushed
¼ cup fresh basil
¼ cup olive oil
Salt and pepper
1 Tbls. fresh oregano

- Preheat oven to 500°.
- Combine all the ingredients, except cheese, in a bowl.  Spread on dough and top with cheese.
- Turn down oven to 425°. Bake for 15-20 minutes, or until very bubbly and crust browned.

# Chutneys, Jams, Sauces, Oils and Butters

The author's parents at the Barnacle, where they honeymooned in
1944

# Faith's Cranberry Chutney

Faith is our wonderful neighbor on Nantucket Island. Several years ago I spent the winter there, and while doing so she shared this recipe with me. I usually triple the recipe so that the chutney can be given as presents at Christmas and throughout the year.

4 cups cranberries
½ cup vinegar
1 cup sugar
2 cups water
1 large red onion, chopped

1 cup walnuts
1 cup currants or raisins
¼ cup fresh ginger, grated
½ teaspoon cloves
½ teaspoon cayenne

♦ In a large pot boil the cranberries, onion, vinegar, sugar and water until thickened.
♦ Stir in the walnuts, currants and spices.
♦ Sterilize canning jars in a boiling pot of water.
♦ Pour the chutney into the jars and cover with melted paraffin, or seal jars.

# Cranberry Orange Sauce

2 cups cranberries
1 cup sugar

2 oranges

♦ Cut the oranges in half and discard the seeds.
♦ Combine all the ingredients in a food processor until there are fine chunks of orange and cranberry.
♦ Pour into a jar or covered bowl and store until ready to use.

# Cranberry Sauce

2 cups cranberries                    1½ cups sugar
2 cups water

- Boil the sugar and water together for 5 minutes.
- Add cranberries. Cook until cranberries pop open. Remove from heat and allow to cool.
- Pour into a jar or bowl and refrigerate until serving time. The sauce will thicken.

# Cranberry Conserve

8 cups cranberries              4 cups sugar
2 cups water                    2 cups walnut pieces
Juice of 2 oranges

- In a large pot cook the water and berries until the berries pop. Add orange juice and sugar. Cook until thickened. Remove from heat and add walnuts.
- Sterilize canning jars. Pour conserve into jars. Seal with paraffin, or seal jars.

# Cranberry Apple Conserve

2 cups apples, peeled, cored and    4 cups sugar
diced                          1 cup walnuts
8 cups cranberries             1 cup raisins
4 cups water                    2 Tbls fresh ginger, grated

- In a large pot combine the apples, cranberries, water and sugar. Bring to a boil.
- Add the walnuts, raisins and ginger. Cook slowly for 5 minutes.
- Sterilize canning jars. Pour the conserve into jars and seal with paraffin, or seal jars.

# Whole Cranberry Sauce

8 cups cranberries
2 cups water
4 cups sugar
4 2-in. cinnamon sticks

24 whole cloves
12 allspice berries
¼ cup fresh ginger

- In a large pot bring all the ingredients to a boil. Simmer for 15 minutes.
- Pour into sterilized jars and seal with paraffin, or seal jars.

# Cranberry Butter

1 stick unsalted butter, softened          ½ cup cranberries, mashed

- In a bowl combine the butter and cranberries.
- Mold into small balls.
- Serve with hot breads or rolls.

# Cranberry Cream

2 cups cranberries
½ cup sugar

2 cups whipping cream

- In a food processor combine cranberries and sugar.
- Whip the cream until a peak forms. Fold in cranberry mixture.
- Spread over pound cake, white cake, or lemon cake as a frosting.
- A variation of this uses 1 stick butter, 8 ounce package cream cheese, 1 package confectioners sugar, 2 teaspoons vanilla and 1 cup cranberries. Combine all ingredients in a bowl and spread over the cake. This is especially good on lemon cake.

# Quince Jam

Quince grow in our front yard in Nantucket. They usually come out too late in the fall for me to pick them, but dear Faith has used them over the years.

1 dozen quince
4 apples, peeled, cored and sliced

Juice and grated rind of 2 oranges
Grated rind of 1 lemon
Sugar

- Rub the fuzz off the quince. Wash and place in a pan. Cover with water. Bring to a boil and simmer for 10 minutes.
- Remove the quince from the pan. Reserve liquid.
- Peel, core and chop the quince.
- Place the quince, orange juice, rinds and apples in the pan.
- Add the reserved liquid until the fruit is covered. Bring to a boil and simmer until fruit is tender.
- Mash or put the fruit in a food processor.
- Measure the fruit. For each cup of fruit add ¾ cup sugar. Heat and bring to a boil. Cook for 10 minutes.
- Pour into sterilized jars and cover with paraffin, or seal tops. Store in cool dry place.

# Beach Plum Jelly

Beach plum jelly is an old Nantucket favorite. For many years cousin Chile Richmond made lots of jams and sold them to family and friends. My mother always made sure we each got a jar in our Christmas stocking.

8 cups beach plums, washed, no leaves or stems

1 cup water
4 cups sugar

- In a large pot simmer the plums in water for about 15-20 minutes.
- Pour the plums into a sieve lined with cheese cloth, place over another pot, and let juice slowly drip through.
- Add the sugar and bring to a boil, stirring until the sugar is dissolved. Remove from the heat and skim off the foam.
- Pour into sterilized jars and seal with paraffin, or seal tops.

# Rose Hip Jam

Rose hips have almost no flavor. Over the years rose hip jam mainly has been made with a lot of sugar and lemon juice for flavor. Rose hips should not be picked until after the first frost.

4 cups rose hips                       Juice of 1 lemon
4 cups sugar                           1 cup water

- Remove the stems and seeds from the rose hips.
- Boil the sugar and water and add the rose hips and lemon juice. Boil for 20 minutes, or until syrup is thickened.
- Pour into hot, sterilized jars and seal with tops or paraffin.

# Little Ga's Grape Conserve

Makes about 12 jars

3 pints grapes                    ½ pound seeded raisins
3 pints sugar                     2 oranges, sliced thin
Scant pint water               1 cup pecans (optional)

- Wash the grapes and press the pulp from the skins using a sieve.
- Cut the oranges in half and remove seeds. Put the oranges through a meat grinder or food processor.
- In a sauce pan heat the grape pulp, orange pulp and sugar (1 cup for each cup of grape pulp), and simmer for 5 minutes, or until tender.
- Add the raisins. Cook until thickened.
- Add nuts.
- Pour into sterilized jars and seal with paraffin.

# Nana's Grape Conserve

6 lbs. Concord grapes
½ pint water
6 cups sugar

½ pound seedless raisins
Juice and rind of 2 oranges
1½ cups walnuts

- Pulp grapes, saving skins. Add water to pulp. In a pan bring to a boil. Strain in a sieve or cheese cloth bag.
- Add skins to juice, then raisins, sugar, orange juice and rind. Boil 20 minutes. After 15 minutes add nuts.
- Pour into jelly glasses and seal with tops or paraffin.


# Mrs. Stonestreet's Apricot Marmalade

4 pounds sugar
1¼ pounds apricots, peeled, pitted, and chopped

¼ pound crystallized ginger
1 large can sliced pineapple, cut up

- In a bowl cover the apricots with water and soak overnight.
- Cut ginger finely and add pineapple in a pot. Add the sugar and apricots and cook for ¾ hour.
- Pour into sterilized jars and cover with paraffin or seal with tops.


# Blueberry Jam

Juice and grated rind of 2 lemons
1½ cups water

4 pints blueberries
7 cups sugar

- In a pot boil the lemon rind and juice and water for 20 minutes, covered.
- Add the blueberries and sugar and cook for another 20 minutes, or until thickened.
- Remove from heat and pour into sterilized jars and seal with paraffin or tops.

# Kay's Red Onion Marmalade

1 Tbls. extra virgin olive oil
1 lb. Red onions, thinly sliced
1 teaspoon light brown sugar
White pepper and salt, to taste

¼ cup red wine vinegar
½ cup Burgandy
½ Tbls. fresh chives, chopped

- Heat olive oil to very hot in a heavy pan. Add onions. Cook over medium heat for 10 minutes.
- Add brown sugar and stir to coat onions. Season with salt and pepper. Continue cooking over medium heat, stirring frequently until onions are golden brown, about 10-15 minutes.
- Add vinegar until it has evaporated.
- Add Burgandy and continue stirring to prevent sticking or burning.
- When red wine has evaporated, taste, correct seasoning and remove from heat.
- The marmalade can be prepared 2 days ahead of meal.

# Kay's Rhubarb Chutney

1 pound rhubarb, diced
½ cup brown sugar, packed
¼ cup cider vinegar
¼ cup raisins
½ teaspoon lemon rind, grated

½ teaspoon ground ginger
¼ teaspoon dry mustard
¼ teaspoon cumin
¼ teaspoon salt

- Combine all the ingredients in a heavy 2 quart pan. Cook on half heat until bubbles form around the edge. Reduce heat to low and simmer 15 minutes.
- Cool and chill.

# Peggy Frantz' Pumpkin Marmalade

Makes about 17 ½ - pint jars

5 pounds pumpkin, after rind is
cut off
12 cups sugar

3 Tbls. ground ginger
3 Tbls. ground cinnamon
6 lemons

- ◆ "Preparing the pumpkin meat is a breeze if you own or borrow the right tools. Otherwise it would be a HUGE job". A heavy sharp knife such as a cheese cleaver takes the rind off easily. – Peggy Frantz.
- ◆ Julienne the pumpkin in strips about ¼" in cross-section. Mix with sugar and spices and let stand overnight.
- ◆ Seed and chop, or grind the lemons, skin and all and cook in water to cover, about 20 minutes.
- ◆ Add to other ingredients. Cook until pumpkin is transparent, about 1 hour.
- ◆ Seal in sterilized jars.

# Peggy' Frantz' Pumpkin Chutney

Use the above recipe for Pumpkin Marmalade, but add before cooking:

12 small white onions, whole or
halved
1 cup vinegar
¼ cup mustard seed

½ pound currants
1 teaspoon salt
½ teaspoon garlic salt
1 oz. fresh ginger, shaved

*Fried Cod*
*Hash Browns*
*Blueberry Muffins*
*Tomato Relish*
*Fresh Fruit*

# Tomato Relish

5 pounds ripe medium tomatoes, peeled and chopped
¼ cup kosher salt
1 cup celery, finely chopped
1 red bell pepper, finely chopped
1 green pepper, finely chopped
1 large onion, finely chopped

½ cup sugar
½ cup mustard seeds
1 teaspoon grated nutmeg
1 teaspoon whole cloves
1 teaspoon cinnamon
1 teaspoon celery seeds
2 cups white vinegar

- Place the tomatoes and salt in a bowl. Let stand one hour. Drain.
- Combine the tomatoes, celery, red bell pepper, green pepper, onion, sugar and vinegar in a large kettle.
- Tie the spices in a cheesecloth bag and add to the kettle. Bring to a boil. Let simmer 30 minutes.
- Discard the spice bag.
- Pour the relish into sterilized jars and seal with paraffin, or tops.

# Corn Relish

8 cups fresh corn kernels
4 cups onion, finely chopped
2 green peppers, finely chopped
2 red bell peppers, finely chopped
2 green chiles, seeded and finely chopped

2 Tbls. celery seed
2 Tbls. mustard seed
1 quart cider vinegar
1 cup sugar
2 Tbls. salt

- Combine all the ingredients in a large pot.
- Stir and bring to a boil. Reduce heat and let simmer for 20 minutes.
- Ladle into sterilized jars and seal with paraffin, or tops.

# Corn Salsa

4 cups fresh cooked corn
2 large tomatoes, chopped
1 red pepper, chopped
2 scallions, chopped
2 jalapeno peppers, seeded and chopped

¼ cup fresh lime juice
2 Tbls. white wine vinegar
2 Tbls. olive oil
½ teaspoon salt
1 teaspoon fresh ground pepper
½ teaspoon cumin

- ◆ Combine all the ingredients in a bowl.
- ◆ Serve with grilled seafood or meat.

# Peach Salsa

2 large peaches, peeled, pitted and chopped very finely
2 scallions, sliced
¼ cup olive oil
2 Tbls. white wine vinegar

2 Tbls. fresh cilantro, chopped
2 Tbls. lime juice
1 green jalapeno, seeded and chopped

- ◆ In a bowl combine all the ingredients.
- ◆ Serve with fish or meat.

# Tartar Sauce

1 cup mayonnaise
2 Tbls. parsley, finely chopped
2 Tbls. chives, chopped
2 Tbls. tarragon, chopped
1 scallion, finely chopped

2 Tbls. capers
2 Tbls. sweet pickle, finely chopped
1 clove garlic, finely chopped

- ◆ Combine all the ingredients in a bowl.
- ◆ Serve with seafood

# Easy Hollandaise

1 stick butter                        ½ lemon
3 egg yolks

- Melt butter in a small saucepan.
- Into food processor put egg yolks. Blend until smooth.
- Slowly pour butter into processor while blending.
- Add juice of the lemon.
- Serve with broccoli, fish, or on Eggs Benedict.

# Bearnaise Sauce

2 Tbls. white wine vinegar        1 stick butter
2 tablespoons white wine          3 egg yolks
1 tablespoon chopped shallots    ½ lemon
1 tablespoon fresh tarragon      Salt and pepper

- Melt the butter and pour into a food processor. Add egg yolks and lemon juice.
- Combine the vinegar, white wine, shallots and tarragon in a small saucepan. Bring to a boil and reduce to about half.
- Serve with beef.

# Pesto

1 large bunch basil leaves        2 cloves garlic
½ cup parmesan cheese           ¼ cup olive oil
¼ cup pine nuts

- Combine all the ingredients in a food processor until the basil is very finely chopped.
- Serve over pasta, chicken, tomatoes, or other dishes.

# Barbecue Sauce

¼ cup peanut butter
½ cup maple syrup or molasses
¾ cup ketchup
¼ cup mustard

1 small onion, chopped
1 Tbls. Worcestershire sauce
Salt and pepper, to taste

- ◆ Combine all the ingredients in a sauce pan. Bring to a boil.
- ◆ Use on chicken or pork.

# Spinach Dressing

½ pound fresh baby spinach
¼ cup olive oil
2 Tbls. balsamic vinegar
1 Tbls. fresh lemon juice

¼ cup pine nuts
2 garlic cloves
Salt and pepper

- ◆ In a food processor combine all the ingredients.
- ◆ This can be used in place of pesto over pasta, or served with chicken or as a salad dressing.

# Herb Salad Dressing

1 cup sugar
¼ cup dry mustard
1 teaspoon salt
4 cloves garlic

1 ½ cups olive oil
1 ½ cups red wine vinegar
¼ cup fresh basil
1 Tbls. marjoram

- ◆ Combine all the ingredients in a food processor.
- ◆ Pour into a jar. Refrigerate.
- ◆ If not using immediately substitute 1 Tbls. dried basil for the fresh.

# Rosemary Oil

1 cup olive oil

¼ cup fresh rosemary, stems removed and rosemary leaves cut in half

- ◆ In a jar combine the rosemary and olive oil.
- ◆ Let sit overnight.
- ◆ Serve, instead of butter, with warm Portuguese or French bread.

# Mrs. Mathews Butter Sauce for Fish

1 stick butter, softened
1 teaspoon salt
¼ teaspoon pepper

1 Tbls. parsley, chopped
1½ Tbls. lemon juice
2 hardboiled eggs, chopped

- ◆ Cream the butter until fluffy and add eggs, salt, pepper, parsley and combine well. Work in lemon juice slowly.
- ◆ Serve with any type of fish.

# Mint Sauce

1 cup mint leaves, crushed
1 cup vinegar

½ cup sugar

- ◆ Combine ingredients in a jar.
- ◆ Store in refrigerator until ready to use.
- ◆ Serve with lamb.

# *Desserts*

**Strawberry and Blueberry Trifle**

*Frozen mousse was introduced to Nantucketers in the 1840s by the William Crosby's at 1 Pleasant Street. They gave a number of dinner parties and were among the leading hosts during the height of the whaling boom. Later the house was to become Jimmy Barker's gallery, and today a private home once again.*

# Strawberry and Blueberry Trifle

Trifle is the most sinfully delicious dessert. My husband doesn't like birthday cakes, but he'll eat trifle instead.

Serves 12

| | |
|---|---|
| 3 dozen ladyfingers | 1 quart strawberries |
| 1 cup Port | 2½ cups heavy cream |
| 1 quart blueberries | 1 cup toasted almonds |

- ♦ In a large clear punch bowl arrange the ladyfingers separately around the side of the bowl. Pour the Port over them so that it can be absorbed.
- ♦ Evenly distribute the fruit over the ladyfingers (reserve several berries for garnish).
- ♦ Pour custard over the fruit. Refrigerate.
- ♦ Lightly whip the cream and spread over the custard.
- ♦ Garnish with almonds and extra strawberries and blueberries.

*Custard*

| | |
|---|---|
| 8 egg yolks | 3½ cups heavy cream |
| ¼ cup sugar | 1 teaspoon vanilla |

- ♦ Whisk the egg yolks and sugar in a bowl.
- ♦ Bring the cream to a boil in a heavy sauce pan. Remove from heat.
- ♦ Slowly pour the egg mixture into the cream, stirring constantly with a wooden spoon.
- ♦ Return the pan to the stove and still stirring heat pan to thicken the custard. Do not allow to boil.
- ♦ Remove from heat and stir in vanilla. Refrigerate before using.

# Blueberry and Strawberry Tart

*Pastry*

2 cups flour
Pinch of salt
¾ cup sugar

1 stick unsalted butter
1 egg yolk

- Preheat oven to 375°.
- In a food processor blend all the ingredients until a ball forms. Remove and shape into a ball. Place in a bowl. Cover and refrigerate for 1 hour.
- Roll out the pastry into a 10" fluted tin pan.
- Bake for 15 minutes in oven. Remove from oven and let cool.

*Filling*

1¾ cup mascarpone
2 Tbls. sugar
½ teaspoon vanilla
Rind of 1 orange, grated

2 cups strawberries
2 cups blueberries
½ cup red currant jam
2 teaspoons fresh orange juice

- In a bowl combine the mascarpone, sugar, vanilla, and orange rind. Pour into pie crust. Top with fruit.
- In a small saucepan heat the jam and orange juice. Pour over the berries.
- If not using immediately refrigerate.
- This can be served with whipped cream or ice cream.

# Key Lime Pie with Blueberries

Key lime pie is a refreshing way to finish off a good seafood dinner. This is also a very easy recipe.

9" graham cracker pie crust

+ Bake pie crust in 400° oven for 10 minutes or until slightly browned.

*Filling*

½ cup key lime juice
1 can condensed sweetened milk
3 eggs, separated

1 cup blueberries
¼ cup blueberry jam

+ In small mixing bowl beat egg whites until firm.
+ Beat egg yolks in a separate bowl. Add condensed milk and key lime juice.
+ Pour key lime mixture into cooled pie crust.
+ In a bowl combine the blueberry jam and blueberries. Gently spoon on top of key lime mixture.
+ Top with beaten egg whites.
+ Place under broiler for about 10 seconds (keep an eye on this).
+ Store in refrigerator until used. Best served same day as made, though it can be frozen.


# Easy Blueberry Dessert

Serves 4

1 quart blueberries
Juice of 1 lime

1 cup brown sugar
½ pint sour cream

+ Place the blueberries in a serving dish and sprinkle with the lime juice.
+ Serve the brown sugar and sour cream in separate bowls with the blueberries.

# Ga's Blueberry Grunt

Serves 4-6

2 cups blueberries                1 cup water
1 cup sugar                       2 cups Bisquick

- ◆ Cook the blueberries, sugar and ¼ cup water till soft.
- ◆ In a bowl combine the Bisquick and rest of the water to make a soft dough.
- ◆ Drop the Bisquick dough by the forkful into the blueberries and boil 10 minutes uncovered, then 10 minutes covered.


# Blueberry Pie

4 cups blueberries                ¼ teaspoon nutmeg
2 Tbls. flour                     1 Tbls. lemon juice
¾ cup sugar                       2 teaspoons butter

- ◆ In a bowl combine the flour, sugar, nutmeg, and lemon juice.
- ◆ Fill the crust with the blueberries. Top with flour mixture. Top with lattice upper crust. Brush top with milk.
- ◆ Bake for 30 minutes at 450°, and then at 350° for 10 minutes.
- ◆ Serve with ice cream, whipped cream, or rum sauce.
- ◆ Strawberries, blackberries, raspberries, or peaches can be substituted for the blueberries.

*Pie Crust*

2 cups flour                      ½ cup cold water
½ stick butter                    ¼ cup sugar
3 ounces cream cheese

- ◆ Combine all crust ingredients in a food processor.
- ◆ Divide dough into two balls. On a floured board roll out one ball into the shape of a 9" shell. Put in a pie plate.
- ◆ Roll the remaining dough into a rectangle and cut into strips to make a lattice work top for the pie.

# Blueberry Peach Brown Betty

Serves 4-6

| | |
|---|---|
| 8 peaches | ¼ cup brown sugar |
| 1 pint blueberries | ½ cup flour |
| Grated rind of an orange | ½ cup old fashioned oats |
| Juice of ½ lemon | ½ stick butter, melted |
| ¼ cup sugar | 1 Tbls. cinnamon |

- Preheat oven to 350°.
- Peel, pit and slice peaches. Wash the blueberries. Place peaches, blueberries and grated orange rind in a baking dish. Sprinkle with lemon juice.
- In a bowl combine the sugars, flour, oats, cinnamon and butter. Cover the fruit with crumb mixture.
- Bake for 30 minutes.
- Serve with vanilla or butter pecan ice cream, or whipped cream.
- 1 cup pecans or walnuts can be added to fruit.
- Pears or blackberries can be substituted for the fruit.

# Honeyed Rum Blueberries

Serves 4

| | |
|---|---|
| 1 pint blueberries | ½ cup rum |
| ½ cup honey | 1 pint vanilla ice cream |

- In a bowl combine the rum and honey. Gently stir in the blueberries, coating them with the mixture.
- Fill four bowls with ice cream and top with blueberries.

# Elsie Good's Blueberry Buckle Cake

Elsie Good was a friend of Little Ga's and shared this recipe with her.

*Batter*

½ cup butter
½ cup sugar
1 egg, beaten
2 cups flour

2 teaspoons baking powder
½ teaspoon salt
½ cup milk
2 cups blueberries

- ◆ Cream together the butter and sugar. Add the egg, flour, baking powder, salt and milk.
- ◆ Spread in a 9 x 13 baking dish. Spoon the blueberries over the top. Then topping. Bake for 1 hour.
- ◆ Serve with cream, whipped cream or ice cream.

*Topping*

½ cup flour
½ cup sugar

½ teaspoon cinnamon
½ stick butter

- ◆ Combine ingredients in a bowl until a crumbly consistency.
- ◆ Sprinkle over the blueberries.

# Blueberry Cakes

1 stick butter
½ cup sugar
1 teaspoon grated lemon rind
2 eggs, beaten

1 cup flour
½ cup whipping cream
1 cup blueberries
Powdered sugar

- ◆ Preheat the oven to 375°.
- ◆ Cream the butter, sugar and lemon rind in a bowl. Gradually beat in the eggs, then flour.
- ◆ Pour into a greased muffin tin. Bake 15-20 minutes or until golden.
- ◆ Let cool.
- ◆ Top with whipped cream, blueberries and a dusting of powdered sugar.

# Little Ga's Blueberry Goodies

*Berry Mixture*

4 cups blueberries
¾ cup sugar

3 Tbls. cornstarch
2 Tbls. lemon juice

- ♦ Preheat oven to 350°.
- ♦ Combine the ingredients and put into a 9" baking dish.
- ♦ Spoon the topping over the mixture.
- ♦ Bake for 20-25 minutes, until topping is just browned.
- ♦ Serve with whipped cream or ice cream.

*Topping*

½ cup old fashioned oats
¾ cup flour
½ cup brown sugar
½ cup sugar

½ teaspoon vanilla
Dash of salt
½ stick butter

- ♦ In a bowl combine the dry ingredients and cut in butter and vanilla.

# Chocolate Strawberries

Serves 8-10

2 quarts large strawberries

½ pint whipping cream, whipped

*Chocolate Sauce*

1 pkg. chocolate mini morsels
½ cup sugar

½ cup milk
½ teaspoon vanilla

- ♦ In a saucepan melt the sauce ingredients and bring to a boil until thickened.
- ♦ Serve in a bowl and allow guests to dip strawberries in the chocolate sauce and/or whipped cream.

# Ann Burwell's Strawberry Pie

1 cup sugar
2 Tbls. cornstarch
2 cups water

1 3 ounce pkg. strawberry jello
1 quart fresh strawberries
1 pie crust, baked

- ◆ In a pan stir together sugar, cornstarch and water. Cook until clear.
- ◆ Add jello. Remove from heat and cool until thickened.
- ◆ Hull the strawberries and leave whole. Add the strawberries to the jello. Refrigerate until partially set.
- ◆ Pour into pie shell and refrigerate.

# Cranberry Custard Pie

1 cup sugar
2 cups light cream
2 egg yolks, beaten

1 teaspoon vanilla
9" pie crust
2 cups cranberries

*Custard*

- ◆ In a sauce pan heat the cream to boiling. Remove from heat and let cool.
- ◆ Gradually add the eggs and then the vanilla. Beat until thickened.
- ◆ Refrigerate for 2 hours. Spoon into the pie crust.
- ◆ In a bowl combine the cranberries and sugar. Spoon over the custard.
- ◆ Refrigerate pie until served.

*Pie Crust*

1½ cups graham cracker crumbs
¼ cup butter, melted

¼ cup sugar

- ◆ Preheat oven to 400°.
- ◆ In a bowl combine all the pie crust ingredients. Press into a 9" pie plate. Bake for 10 minutes or until just browned. Cool.
- ◆ This is also very good using crushed chocolate wafers instead of the graham crackers.

# Cranberry Pie

4 cups cranberries
1 ½ cups sugar
2 Tbls. butter, melted
2 Tbls. flour

3 Tbls. water
1 cup pecans
2 pie crusts

- ◆ Preheat oven to 350°.
- ◆ In a bowl combine all the ingredients except pie crust.
- ◆ Line a pie plate with one crust and pour the cranberry mixture on top.
- ◆ Cut the other pie crust into strips and make a lattice work top for the pie.
- ◆ Bake for about 30 minutes or until crust is just browned.

# Cranberry Betty

Serves 4-6

4 cups cranberries
Juice of one orange
Rind of one orange, grated
1 cup raisins
1 cup white sugar
1 cup water

½ cup flour
1 cup old fashioned oats
½ cup brown sugar
2 teaspoons cinnamon
1 stick butter, melted

- ◆ Preheat oven to 375°.
- ◆ In a baking dish combine the cranberries, orange juice, orange rind, raisins, and white sugar.
- ◆ In a separate bowl combine the flour, oats, brown sugar, cinnamon and butter. Pour over the cranberries.
- ◆ Bake ½ hour.
- ◆ Serve with whipped cream or ice cream.
- ◆ 1 cup walnuts or pecans can be substituted for the raisins.

# Cranberry Cake

2 cups flour
½ cup sugar
1 teaspoon cinnamon
½ stick butter

2 apples, cored and diced
1 cup cranberries
¾ cup apple juice
1 jar cranberry jelly

- Preheat the oven to 350°.
- In a bowl combine the flour, sugar, cinnamon and butter. Stir in the cranberries, 1 apple and apple juice.
- Spoon the mixture into a greased ring.
- Bake for 35-40 minutes, or a toothpick comes out dry. Turn out of pan and let cool on a cake plate.
- Heat the cranberry jelly in a sauce pan and pour over the cake just before serving. Garnish with other apple and cranberries.

# Cranberry Roll

4 cups cranberries
½ cup brown sugar
½ cup white sugar

1 cup pecans
½ stick butter, melted

- In a bowl combine all the above ingredients.
- Spread the cranberry mixture evenly over the dough leaving about ¼" on each edge.
- Roll lengthwise and seal at the ends. Place on a greased cookie sheet.
- Bake about 45 minutes or until browned on outside.
- Remove from oven and dust with granulated or powdered sugar.
- Cut into 2 inch strips.
- Serve hot with ice cream or whipped cream.

*Pastry*

1 ½ cups flour
1 ½ sticks butter

¼ cup cold water
¼ cup sugar

- Preheat oven to 325°.
- In a food processor combine the pastry ingredients until a ball forms.
- On a floured board roll out into the shape of a 12" x 8" rectangle.

# Chocolate Cranberries

1 pound cranberries
1 cup sugar

½ cup cream
4 ounces semi sweet chocolate

- Combine the ingredients, except cranberries, in a sauce pan and stir until thickened.
- Dip the cranberries individually in the chocolate. Place on a platter.
- Refrigerate if not using immediately. Serve in a bowl.

# Cranberry Parfait

Rum raisin ice cream
Cranberries

Whipped cream

- In parfait glasses layer the ice cream and cranberries. Top with whipped cream.

# Fruit with Sour Cream Dip

Serves 8-10

1 pound strawberries
4 peaches, peeled, cored and thickly sliced

4 apples, peeled, cored and sliced
1 pint raspberries or blackberries

- Arrange the fruit on a platter with the dip in the center.

*Dip*

2 cups sour cream
¼ cup honey

¼ cup mint leaves

- Combine the ingredients in a bowl and serve with the fruit.

# Summer Fruit

Serves at least 20

| | |
|---|---|
| 1 watermelon | 1 cantaloupe |
| 4 large plums | 1 quart strawberries, hulled |
| 4 large peaches | 1 pint blueberries |
| 4 apricots | 1 cup kirsh |
| 2 oranges | 1 Tbls. fresh ginger |
| 1 pound seedless grapes | Mint leaves |
| 1 honeydew melon | |

- Cut the watermelon in the shape of a basket.
- With a melon baller remove the watermelon and put in a large bowl.
- Cut the cantaloupe and honey dew melons in half and remove melon with a melon baller. Put into a bowl with the watermelon.
- Peel, seed and slice the oranges, plums, peaches and apricots. Also place in bowl.
- Add strawberries and blueberries. Cover with kirsh and sprinkle with fresh ginger. Refrigerate.
- When ready to serve put all the fruit in the hollowed out watermelon. Garnish with mint.
- Rum can be substituted for the kirsh.

# Peach Melba

Serves 4

| | |
|---|---|
| 2 cups fresh raspberries | 4 large peaches |
| 1 Tbls. sugar | Vanilla ice cream |
| Juice of 1 lemon | |

- Place the raspberries, sugar and lemon in a food processor until smooth.
- Dip the peaches into a pot of boiling water, and remove skins. Cut in half. Remove pit, and slice thinly.
- Place two scoops vanilla ice cream in each bowl.
- Top with peach slices and pour raspberry sauce on top. Serve immediately.

# Peach Blueberry Crisp

Serves 4

4 large peaches, peeled, pitted and sliced
1 pint blueberries
1 cup sugar
1 cup flour

½ cup old-fashioned oats
½ cup milk
1 teaspoon vanilla
1 stick butter

- ◆ Preheat oven to 400°.
- ◆ In a bowl combine the peaches, blueberries and ½ cup sugar. Let stand 15 minutes.
- ◆ Combine flour, oats, milk, and ½ cup sugar in another bowl. Spread the batter in a 8" x 8" baking dish.
- ◆ Top the batter with the fruit mixture.
- ◆ Bake about 45 minutes, until crisp on top.
- ◆ Serve with vanilla or butter pecan ice cream.
- ◆ Apples, pears, raspberries, or blackberries can be substituted for the fruit.

# Spiced Apples

Serves 4

4 large apples, peeled, cored and sliced
1 cup sugar
½ stick butter

1 teaspoon cinnamon
½ teaspoon ginger
¼ teaspoon nutmeg
Butter pecan or vanilla ice cream

- ◆ In a skillet melt the butter and add the apple slices. Saute 10 minutes, or until the apples are tender. Stir in the spices.
- ◆ Serve hot over ice cream.
- ◆ Pecans, walnuts or raisins can be added to the apples.

# Apple Torte

1 egg
¾ cup sugar
¾ cup apples, peeled, cored, and sliced
1 teaspoon baking powder

½ cup flour
Pinch of salt
¼ teaspoon almond extract
¼ cup walnuts, chopped

- ♦ In a bowl beat the egg slightly. Add sugar and apple slices. Stir in remaining ingredients until well mixed.
- ♦ Pour into a greased 8" x 8" baking dish. Bake for 25 minutes.
- ♦ Serve with whipped cream or ice cream.

# Apple Crumb Pie

*Pie Crust*

1¼ cups flour
1 stick butter

¼ cup water
2 Tbls. sugar

- ♦ Preheat oven to 375°.
- ♦ In a food processor combine all the ingredients until a ball is formed.
- ♦ Roll out into 9" pie shape and place in pie pan.

*Filling*

¼ cup brown sugar
½ cup flour
½ stick butter, melted
6 apples, peeled, cored and sliced

¾ cup sugar
1 teaspoon cinnamon
1 Tbls lemon juice
½ cup chopped pecans

- ♦ In a bowl combine the brown sugar, flour and butter.
- ♦ In a large bowl combine the apples, sugar, cinnamon, lemon juice and pecans. Spoon into pie crust.
- ♦ Sprinkle the brown sugar topping over the apples.
- ♦ Bake for 45 minutes or until browned.
- ♦ Serve with whipped cream or ice cream.

# Apple Cranberry Pie

9" graham cracker pie crust

*Filling*

3 cups apples, peeled, cored and thinly sliced
Juice of 1 lemon
2 cups fresh cranberries
½ stick butter
¼ cup sugar
¼ cup brown sugar

¼ cup flour
½ teaspoon nutmeg
½ teaspoon ground ginger
1 Tbls. cinnamon
¼ teaspoon ground cloves
½ teaspoon ground allspice

- Preheat oven to 350°.
- Combine all the ingredients in a bowl, except pie crust.
- Pour ingredients into pie crust.
- Bake 45 minutes.

# Apple Crumble

Serves 4

4 Granny Smith apples, peeled, cored and sliced
1 pint raspberries
Juice of 1 lemon
½ cup flour
½ cup old fashioned oats

½ cup sugar
½ cup pecans
1 stick butter
¼ teaspoon nutmeg
½ teaspoon cinnamon
Whipping cream

- Preheat oven to 375°.
- Arrange the apple slices in a buttered 8" x 8" baking dish. Sprinkle the lemon juice over apples.
- Carefully place the raspberries on the apples.
- In a bowl combine the flour, pecans, oatmeal and sugar. Cut in the butter. Add the nutmeg and cinnamon. Pour over the fruit.
- Bake 25 minutes or until golden.
- Serve with whipped cream or ice cream.

# Blackberry Cheesecake

*Crust*

1½ cups chocolate wafers,
crumbled

½ stick butter, melted
¼ cup sugar

- ♦ In a food processor combine all the ingredients. Line a 9" pie plate with the chocolate mixture.

*Filling*

1 pint blackberries
½ cup blackberry preserves
16 ounces cream cheese
2 eggs

½ cup sugar
1 Tbls. grated lemon peel
1 Tbls. lemon juice
½ teaspoon vanilla

- ♦ Preheat oven to 350°.
- ♦ Combine the blackberries and blackberry preserves. Spoon into pie crust.
- ♦ Beat together the cream cheese, sugar, lemon juice, lemon peel, vanilla and eggs. Pour over blackberries.
- ♦ Bake 1 hour, or until set.

# Rhubarb Pie

2 9" pie crusts
½ cup pecans
2 Tbls. fresh ginger

3 cups rhubarb
½ cup brown sugar

- ♦ Preheat oven to 350°.
- ♦ In a bowl combine the rhubarb, brown sugar, pecans and ginger. Pour into one pie crust.
- ♦ Cut the other crust into strips and make a lattice top on the pie.
- ♦ Bake for 40 minutes.

# Rhubarb Strawberry Pie

9" pie crust

*Filling*

1 pint strawberries
3 cups rhubarb, cut into ½ inch pieces

1 Tbls. cornstarch
¼ cup sugar

- ♦ Preheat oven to 350°.
- ♦ In a bowl combine the strawberries, rhubarb, cornstarch and sugar.
- ♦ Line the pie crust with the mixture. Spread the topping over this.
- ♦ Bake for 40 minutes.

*Topping*

½ cup flour
½ cup sugar
½ stick butter, softened

½ teaspoon cinnamon
¼ teaspoon nutmeg

- ♦ Combine all the ingredients in a bowl.

# Honey Pears

Serves 4-6

6 large ripe pears
½ pound Stilton cheese, cut in slices

½ cup honey

- ♦ Preheat oven to 350°.
- ♦ Slice the pears in half and remove core. Place cut side up in oven for 20 minutes.
- ♦ Remove and top with slices of Stilton and drizzle with honey.
- ♦ Serve warm or chilled.

# Lemon Sabayon with Berries

Serves 4

*Sabayon*

3 eggs                                    ½ cup lemon juice
½ cup sugar                               ¼ cup unsalted butter, softened

- ◆ In the top of a double boiler whisk together the eggs, sugar and lemon juice, stirring for 20-25 minutes until thickened. Remove from heat and add butter.
- ◆ Now place top of double boiler in a bowl of ice water and whisk once again until thickened. Refrigerate.

1 pint raspberries                        ¼ cup confectioners' sugar
1 pint blackberries                       4 sprigs mint
¼ cup dark rum

- ◆ Set aside 8 berries to garnish the top of each dessert. Combine the confectioners' sugar, rum and rest of the berries.
- ◆ Fill the bottom of four large wine glasses or parfait glasses with ½ the sabayon.
- ◆ Top with ½ fruit and sugar. Repeat layer.
- ◆ Garnish with reserved fruit and mint leaves.
- ◆ Strawberries or blueberries can be substituted for the raspberries and blackberries.

# Lemon Blueberry Souffle

Serves 6

Grated rind of 1 lemon
½ cup lemon juice
1 package gelatin
4 eggs, separated

1 cup sugar
½ teaspoon vanilla
1 pint whipping cream

- ◆ In a small pan heat the lemon juice and sprinkle in the gelatin to dissolve. Cool.
- ◆ In a bowl combine the lemon rind, egg yolks, sugar and vanilla until creamy. Stir in the gelatin.
- ◆ In another bowl beat the egg whites until peaks form. Fold the gelatin mixture into egg whites.
- ◆ Pour into a souffle dish and freeze for two hours.
- ◆ Serve on individual plates with blueberry sauce.
- ◆ Extra whipped cream makes for a sinfully delicious dessert.

*Sauce*

2 cups blueberries

¼ cup sugar

- ◆ In a saucepan heat the blueberries and sugar until the juices run.
- ◆ Blackberries, cranberries or strawberries can be substituted for the blueberries.
- ◆ This also is very good with a ¼ cup rum or Cointreau added.

# Strawberries Romanoff

Some of the Romanov family from London have spent time on Nantucket, so it is appropriate to include this sinfully elegant dessert.

Serves 4

| | |
|---|---|
| 1 pound strawberries | 2 Tbls. apricot jam |
| ½ cup sugar | 1 Tbls. water |
| ¼ cup Grand Marnier | 2 squares semisweet chocolate |
| 1 cup heavy cream | 4 mint leaves or rose petals |
| ½ teaspoon vanilla | |

- ◆ Wash the strawberries and remove the stems. Set aside 2 strawberries. Finely chop the rest of the berries and place in a bowl. Toss with the sugar and Grand Marnier.
- ◆ In a bowl whisk together the cream and vanilla until stiff. Add ½ the strawberries.
- ◆ In the bottom of 4 parfait glasses place the strawberries with Grand Marnier.
- ◆ Top with cream and strawberries. Refrigerate.
- ◆ In a saucepan bring the water and jam to a boil to make the glaze.
- ◆ Cut the 2 strawberries that had been set aside in half, lengthwise. Coat with apricot glaze.
- ◆ Garnish each parfait with a strawberry.
- ◆ Melt the chocolate in a sauce pan over a low flame.
- ◆ Dip the mint leaves in the chocolate and place on waxed paper.
- ◆ Place in refrigerator for 5 minutes. Place one leaf on each dessert.

# Pavlova

Pavlova is the national dish of Australia. However it uses the wonderful fruits of a Nantucket summer and is a treat anywhere.

Serves 4-6

3 egg whites
1 cup sugar
1 teaspoon cornstarch
1 teaspoon white wine vinegar
¼ cup toasted almonds
1 cup whipping cream

1 Tbls. orange juice
2 large ripe peaches or nectarines, peeled, pitted and sliced
2 cups raspberries
2 Tbls. red currant jelly, warmed

- ◆ Preheat the oven to 275°. Lightly grease a cookie sheet. Place a parchment sheet on the cookie sheet.
- ◆ In a bowl beat the egg whites until peaks form. Whisk in the sugar 1 Tbls. at a time. Add the cornstarch and vinegar. Spoon the meringue onto the parchment sheet in about an 8" circle. (Individual meringues also can be made). Bake for about 1¼-1½ hours until crisp. Cool. Transfer to a serving platter.
- ◆ Whip the cream and orange juice until peaks form. Spoon on the meringue.
- ◆ Top with the fruit and drizzle the jelly over the top. Serve immediately.

# Little Ga's Indian Tapioca Pudding

4 cups milk
3 Tbls. yellow cornmeal
½ cup molasses
½ cup brown sugar
½ cup cold water
½ teaspoon salt

1 teaspoon cinnamon
2 Tbls. butter
1 egg, beaten
3 Tbls. pearl tapioca, soaked in cold water

- ◆ Preheat oven to 325°.
- ◆ Bring 3 cups of milk and the cornmeal to a boil in a sauce pan. Add the other cup of milk and the remaining ingredients.
- ◆ Pour into a buttered 1½ quart casserole dish.
- ◆ Bake for 3 hours, stirring 2-3 times during the first hour of baking.
- ◆ Serve warm, topped with whipped cream or ice cream.

# Indian Pudding

4 cups milk
1 cup yellow cornmeal
2 eggs, beaten
½ cup sugar
¾ cup molasses
½ teaspoon salt

½ teaspoon cinnamon
¼ teaspoon ground cloves
½ teaspoon ground ginger
¼ teaspoon ground allspice
¼ teaspoon ground nutmeg

- ◆ Preheat oven to 325°
- ◆ Bring the milk to a boil and add the cornmeal. Stir until thickened. Let cool.
- ◆ Stir in remaining ingredients.
- ◆ Pour into a buttered baking dish. Bake 2 hours.
- ◆ Serve hot with ice cream.

# Pumpkin Cheesecake

*Crust*

3 cups ginger snaps
½ cup sugar

½ cup butter, melted

- ◆ Combine the ingredients and press into 2 pie plates.

*Filling*

16 ounces cream cheese
1 cup heavy cream
1 cup pumpkin
1 cup sugar
4 egg yolks
4 egg whites, beaten until stiff

3 tablespoons flour
1 teaspoon vanilla
1 teaspoon cinnamon
1 teaspoon ginger
½ teaspoon fresh grated nutmeg

- ◆ Combine all ingredients except egg whites. Fold in egg whites.
- ◆ Pour filling into 2 crusts.
- ◆ Bake at 325° for one hour.

# Apple Pudding

Serves 8

2 eggs
2 cups sugar
2 cups flour
1 teaspoon baking powder
2 teaspoons baking soda

2 teaspoons cinnamon
¼ teaspoon allspice
4 cups apples, peeled, cored and diced.
¾ cup pecans or walnuts

- Preheat oven to 325°.
- In a bowl beat the eggs until fluffy and add sugar. Add dry ingredients. With fork toss in the apples and pecans.
- Pour into an 8" square pan. Bake 50 minutes.
- Serve with ice cream, whipped cream, or rum sauce.

*Rum Sauce*

1 cup water
1 stick butter
1 cup sugar
2 Tbls. flour

½ teaspoon salt
2 teaspoons vanilla
¼ cup rum

- In a saucepan bring all the ingredients to a boil. Stir until thickened.
- Serve over the apple pudding.

# Baked Apples

Serves 4

4 apples, cored
1 cup cranberries
1 Tbls. cinnamon
¼ cup brown sugar

¼ cup sugar
1 stick butter, melted
½ cup dark rum

- Preheat oven to 350°.
- In a bowl combine all the ingredients, except apples.
- Stuff the apples with the cranberry mixture.
- Bake for 30 minutes.
- Serve with ice cream or whipped cream.

# Apple Cake

1½ cups vegetable oil
2 cups sugar
3 eggs, beaten
3 cups flour
1 teaspoon baking soda
1 teaspoon baking powder
1 teaspoon salt

1 teaspoon cinnamon
1 teaspoon nutmeg
1 cup chopped nuts
3 cups chopped apples
1 cup raisins
2 teaspoons vanilla

♦ Cream the oil and sugar. Add eggs, and then dry ingredients. The batter will be very heavy.
♦ Stir in the nuts, apples, raisins and vanilla.
♦ Pour into well greased tube pan.
♦ Bake for 1½ hours.
♦ This is better if aged a day.

# Pound Cake

Makes 2 loaf cakes

2 sticks butter
2 cups sugar
4 egg yolks
3 cups sifted cake flour
½ teaspoon salt
2 teaspoons baking powder

1 cup milk
½ teaspoon lemon extract
½ teaspoon almond extract
1 teaspoon lemon rind, grated
4 egg whites

♦ Preheat oven to 350°.
♦ Cream the butter and add the sugar. Add the egg yolks one at a time, beating well. Add flour, baking powder, salt, alternating with milk. Add the lemon and vanilla extracts, and lemon rind.
♦ Beat the egg whites until stiff and fold them into batter.
♦ Pour into two loaf pans, which have been lined with wax paper and greased with butter.
♦ Bake for 45 minutes.
♦ This is delicious served with ice cream, strawberries, blueberries, or whipped cream.

# Plum Pudding

1½ cups flour
½ teaspoon soda
½ teaspoon salt
½ teaspoon cinnamon
½ teaspoon cloves
½ teaspoon ground allspice

1 cup chopped suet
½ cup apple, chopped and cored
1 cup raisins
½ cup currants
½ cup molasses
½ cup cold water.

- ◆ Combine all ingredients in a large mixing bowl. Place in a container, such as a coffee can or ovenproof bowl that will fit in a pressure cooker. Cover with wax paper.
- ◆ Cook in pressure cooker under pressure for 40 minutes. Cool.
- ◆ Serve with hard sauce or brandy sauce.

# Fresh Fruit Compote

Serves 10-12

1 cup sugar
¾ cup water
2 2-inch cinnamon sticks
¼ teaspoon ground cloves
¼ teaspoon whole allspice
3 large apples, peeled, cored and thinly sliced

3 large pears, peeled, cored, and thinly sliced
3 large oranges, peeled and sectioned
1 pound green grapes
1 pound strawberries
Mint leaves

- ◆ In a sauce pan combine the sugar and water. Add the cinnamon sticks, cloves and allspice. Bring to a boil.
- ◆ Add the apples and pears. Remove the spices. Chill.
- ◆ When ready to serve add the oranges, grapes and strawberries.
- ◆ Garnish with mint leaves.

# Mrs. Barney's Plum Cake

The date on this recipe is October 28, 1940, given to my grandmother by an old Hopedale friend. When I first found the recipe, I puzzled because it had no plums in it. Instead it called for 2 cups raisins that had been boiled the day before. We wanted to call it raisin cake, but did try plums, instead of raisins and it worked. Canned plums can be substituted, but please drain juice before using in the cake, or substitute the juice for the milk. This makes for a sweeter cake. There is no frosting mentioned for the cake, but a cream cheese frosting would be an added touch.

3 cups sugar
2 sticks butter
4 eggs, beaten
1 cup milk
½ teaspoon baking soda
½ teaspoon cloves

½ teaspoon allspice
1 teaspoon cinnamon
½ teaspoon nutmeg
4 cups flour
2 cups plums, peeled, pitted and cubed

- Preheat oven to 350°
- In a bowl cream together the sugar and butter. Add the other ingredients until well blended.
- Pour into 2 loaf pans.
- Bake for about 1 hour, or until a toothpick comes out dry.

# Ginger Mousse

1 quart heavy cream
2 Tbls. chopped fresh ginger
½ cup coconut
1 cup chopped pecans

½ cup Drambuie
2 Tbls. Scotch
1 box ginger snaps

- In a bowl beat the cream until peaks are formed. Fold in next five ingredients, one at a time. Mix well.
- In a large souffle dish place a layer of ginger snaps. Alternate layers with cream mixture until cream in gone. Last layer will be cream mixture. Make thick layers.
- Cover with plastic wrap.
- Refrigerate overnight.

# Gingerbread

½ cup butter
½ cup sugar
1 egg
2 ½ cups flour
1 ½ teaspoons baking soda
½ teaspoon salt

1 ¼ teaspoon ginger
1 teaspoon cinnamon
½ teaspoon cloves
½ teaspoon allspice
1 cup molasses
1 cup boiling water

- Preheat oven to 350°.
- In a bowl cream butter and add sugar. Beat in the egg.
- In another bowel combine molasses and boiling water.
- Combine butter and molasses mixtures. Gradually add rest of ingredients until well mixed.
- Pour into a 9 x 9 pan.
- Bake 50-60 minutes.
- During the summer add 1 cup blueberries for variety.

# Cracker Pie

16 single saltine crackers, crushed
1 cup sugar
½ teaspoon baking powder

¾ cup chopped walnuts or pecans
3 egg whites, beaten stiff
2 Tbls. butter

- Preheat oven to 350°.
- Put the butter in a 9" pie plate and place in oven to melt.
- In a bowl combine the crushed saltines, sugar, nuts, and baking powder. Fold in the egg whites.
- Pour into buttered pan.
- Bake for 25-30 minutes.
- Serve with whipped cream, custard and strawberries.

# Aunt Lou's Spice Cake

2 cups brown sugar
1 stick butter
3 eggs, separated
1 cup milk
1 teaspoon soda
2 cups flour
2 teaspoons cinnamon

2 teaspoons allspice
1 teaspoon vanilla
¼ teaspoon salt
1 teaspoon baking powder
1 cup raisins
½ cup walnuts or pecans

- ♦ Preheat oven to 350°.
- ♦ In a bowl cream the sugar and butter. Add the egg yolks, milk, soda, flour, cinnamon, allspice, vanilla, salt, baking powder, raisins and walnuts.
- ♦ In a separate bowl beat the egg whites until stiff. Fold into the batter.
- ♦ Bake for 1 hour. Cool.
- ♦ Frost with cream cheese frosting.
- ♦ 1 cup sliced apples or applesauce can be added to the batter.

*Frosting*

1 box confectioner's sugar
1 stick butter

8 ounces cream cheese
2 teaspoons vanilla

- ♦ In a bowl beat together the butter and cream cheese.
- ♦ Add sugar and vanilla and beat until smooth.

# Tia Maria Parfait

For all you coffee lovers!

Rum
Coffee ice cream
Tia Maria

Whipped Cream
Cherries

- ♦ In each parfait glass put 1 tablespoon rum in the bottom.
- ♦ Then put in coffee ice cream, pour some Tia Maria over this.
- ♦ Top with whipped cream and a cherry.

# Crepes Suzette

Makes 8

*Crepes*

| | |
|---|---|
| 1 cup flour | 1 egg yolk |
| 1 Tbls. sugar | 1¼ cups milk |
| Pinch of salt | Butter |
| 1 egg | |

- ♦ Combine the flour, sugar and salt in a bowl. Make a well and crack the egg and extra yolk into flour. Gradually beat in milk. Chill for 30 minutes.
- ♦ In a crepe pan melt some butter Pour in a large spoonful of batter so it reaches edge of pan. Cook until just browned. Flip. Repeat with rest of batter.
- ♦ Set aside crepes on a plate.

*Sauce*

| | |
|---|---|
| 2 large oranges | ¼ cup Grand Marnier |
| ½ stick butter | 1 Tbls. brandy |
| ½ cup light brown sugar | |

- ♦ Grate the rind from the orange and reserve about 1 Tbls of the rind. Squeeze both oranges.
- ♦ Melt the butter in a large skillet. Heat the sugar with the rind and juice until dissolved and bubbling.
- ♦ Fold each crepe into quarters. Add to the pan one at a time and coat in the sauce. Fold again and coat.
- ♦ Pour the Grand Marnier and brandy over the crepes.
- ♦ Cook for 2 minutes more.
- ♦ Sprinkle with the remaining orange rind. Serve immediately.

# Blueberry Bar Cookies

1 cup butter
1 cup sugar
1 cup flour
1 cup quick cooking oats

½ cup brown sugar
1 cup blueberries
½ cup blueberry preserves

- ♦ Preheat oven to 375°.
- ♦ In a large bowl combine the flour, sugars, oats and butter.
- ♦ Press ½ of this mixture into the bottom of a buttered 9" inch square baking dish. Top with blueberry preserves and blueberries. Spoon rest of batter over the blueberries.
- ♦ Bake for 20-25 minutes or until golden brown.
- ♦ Cool and cut into bars.

# Pumpkin Chocolate Brownies

2 sticks butter
4 ounces semi-sweet chocolate
4 eggs
2 cups sugar

1 cup flour
1 teaspoon vanilla
1 cup walnuts or pecans

- ♦ Preheat oven to 350°.
- ♦ Melt the butter and chocolate in a sauce pan. Stir in other ingredients.
- ♦ Pour into a 9" x 13' square baking dish.

½ cup pumpkin
3 ounce package cream cheese
¼ cup sugar
1 egg
1 teaspoon vanilla

½ teaspoon cinnamon
½ teaspoon ginger
½ teaspoon nutmeg
2 Tbls. flour

- ♦ Combine all the ingredients in a bowl.
- ♦ Drop by spoonsful over brownie batter. Then swirl with a spatula.
- ♦ Bake 45-50 minutes.

# Little Ga's Rice Flake Cookies

2 sticks butter
1 cup sugar
1 cup brown sugar
2 eggs
1 teaspoon vanilla
2 cups flour

1 teaspoon baking soda
½ teaspoon baking powder
½ teaspoon salt
1 cup coconut
2 cups Rice Krispies

- ◆ Preheat oven to 375°.
- ◆ Cream the butter and sugars.
- ◆ Add the eggs and vanilla and beat until light. Add rest of ingredients.
- ◆ Shape into small balls and place on a greased cookie sheet.
- ◆ Bake for 10 minutes or until just golden.

# Little Ga's Date Nut Bars

When we were growing up, my mother loved to cook date nut bars, but from a mix. I remember they had coconut in them, which can be added to this recipe.

½ stick butter, melted
1 cup sugar
2 eggs, well beaten
¾ cup flour

Pinch of salt
½ teaspoon baking powder
1 cup dates, finely chopped
½ cup walnuts, chopped

- ◆ Preheat oven to 350°.
- ◆ Cream the butter and sugar. Add the eggs.
- ◆ Beat in the rest of the ingredients.
- ◆ Line a 8" x 8" pan with wax paper. Spread the batter in the pan.
- ◆ Bake 15-20 minutes.

# Gingerbread Men and Women

1 cup butter  
1 cup sugar  
½ cup brown sugar  
¼ cup molasses  
3 ½ cups flour  

2 teaspoons soda  
2 teaspoons cinnamon  
1 teaspoon ground ginger  
½ teaspoon cloves  

- ◆ Preheat oven to 375°.
- ◆ Cream the butter and sugars in a large bowl. Add rest of ingredients and mix well. Chill.
- ◆ On a floured board roll out dough, and cut into shapes. (You will need cookie cutters in the shape of men or women).
- ◆ Bake for 8 minutes.

*Now Let Us Praise Fried Pies*

# Molasses Cookies

1 cup butter  
1 cup sugar  
1 egg  
1 cup molasses  
½ cup strong coffee  
4 ½ cups flour  

1 teaspoon soda  
2 teaspoons ground ginger  
2 teaspoons cinnamon  
1 teaspoon ground cloves  
½ teaspoon salt  

- ◆ Preheat oven to 350°.
- ◆ Cream the butter and sugar in a large bowl. Add the egg, molasses, coffee, flour, soda, and spices.
- ◆ Drop by spoonsful onto an ungreased cookie sheet. Bake for 15 minutes.

*Now Let Us Praise Fried Pies*

# Elizabeth Gould's Camptown Brownies

2 eggs
1 cup sugar
1 stick butter
2 oz. unsweetened chocolate
½ cup chocolate morsels

1 teaspoon vanilla
½ cup flour
1 cup small marshmallows
½ cup broken walnuts or pecans

- Beat the eggs until thick and lemon colored. Gradually add the sugar.
- Melt the butter and chocolate. Add to the eggs. Add vanilla, flour, chocolate morsels, nuts and marshmallows.
- Pour into a 9" square greased baking dish.
- Bake for 25 minutes. Cool and cut into squares.

# Mincemeat Cookies

2 sticks butter
2 cups brown sugar
2 eggs
1 cup mincemeat
1 teaspoon powdered instant coffee

3 ½ cups flour
1 teaspoon baking soda
1 teaspoon salt

- Preheat oven to 400°.
- Cream the butter and sugar.
- Add the eggs and beat in the rest of ingredients. Drop by teaspoons on a greased cookie sheet.
- Bake about 8-10 minutes or until browned.

# Index

## A
**Appetizers**
Asparagus in Prosciutto, 37
Baba Ghannooj, 37
Baby Spinach Fingers, 34
Bacon Wrapped Scallops, 23
Baked Clams, 20
Big Ga's Deviled Eggs, 30
Brie and Blue Cheese, 31
Bruschetta, 28
Cheese Puffs, 30
Chicken Pate, 34
Codfish Balls, 24
Crab Mold, 25
Cranberry Chutney Brie, 31
Crudites, 38
Curried Lobster Salad, 19
Deviled Ham Puffs, 28
Fondue, 32
Fried Crab Balls, 25
Gagi's Stuff & Nonsense, 29
Ginger Dip, 38
Herb Dip, 38
Hot Brie and Cranberries, 31
Hummus, 39
Little Neck Clams, 20
Lobster Dip, 19
Lobster Rounds, 19
Mushroom Toasts, 36
Mussels Casino, 21
Nantucket Mussels, 22
Oversea Cocktail Special, 29
Pate, 33
Pate with Walnuts, 34
Pears with Stilton, 32
Raspberry Brie, 30
Salmon Canapes, 27
Salmon Blini, 25
Salmon Mousse, 26
Salmon Roll-ups, 26
Scallops with Dill Sauce
Seafood Baguettes, 27
Smoked Bluefish Pate, 21
Smoked Duck, 33
Smoked Scallops with Pesto
Spiced Nuts, 39
Spinach Cheesecake, 35
Spinach Dip, 35
Swordfish Blini, 24

Vegetable Cheesecake, 36

**Apples**
Apple Cake, 229
Apple Cheddar Muffins, 169
Apple Cranberry Pie, 220
Apple Crumb Pie, 219
Apple Crumble, 220
Apple Pancakes, 177
Apple Pudding, 228
Apple Torte, 219
Baked Apples, 228
Cranberry Apple Punch, 42
Spiced Apples, 218

**Apricots**
Apricot Marmalade, 197
Wild Rice with Apricots, 160

**Asparagus**
Asparagus and Pasta, 154
Asparagus in Prosciutto, 37
Asparagus Salad, 143
Asparagus Tart, 122
Cream of Asparagus Soup, 60
Pasta Primavera, 155
Veal with Asparagus, 101

## B
**Bacon**
Bacon and Cheese Frittata, 175
Chicken and Bacon Sandwiches, 184

**Barbecue Sauce**
Barbecue Sauce, 203

**Beach Plums**
Beach Plum Jelly, 195
Beach Plum Sauce, 98

**Beans**
Black Bean Salsa, 33
Dilly Green Beans, 112
Green Bean Casserole, 110, 111
Green Beans and Apples, 111
Green Beans with Bacon, 112
Pesto Vegetable Pasta, 156

**Beef**
Beef Nantucket, 103
Beef Oscar, 106
Beef Roulade, 105
Beef Tournedoes, 104
Hot Steak Sandwich, 134
Tenderloin, 104, 105

**Beets**
Baby Beet Salad, 140
Beet Salad, 141

**Blackberries**
Blackberry Cheesecake, 221
Lemon Blackberry Souffle, 224
Lemon Sabayon, 223

**Blueberries**
Blueberry Bar Cookies, 235
Blueberry Buckle Cake, 211
Blueberry Cakes, 211
Blueberry Coffee Cake, 169
Blueberry Goodies, 212
Blueberry Grunt, 209
Blueberry Jam, 197
Blueberry Pancakes, 178
Blueberry Peach Brown Betty, 210
Blueberry Pie, 209
Blueberry Strawberry Tart, 207
Blueberry Waffles, 178
Easy Blueberry Dessert, 208
Honeyed Rum Blueberries, 210
Key Lime Pie with Blueberries, 208
Lemon Blueberry Souffle, 224
Strawberry Blueberry Trifle, 206

**Bluefish**
Baked Bluefish, 77
Smoked Bluefish Pate, 21

**Bread, Biscuits, Coffee Cakes and Pancakes**
Apple Cheddar Muffins, 169
Apricot Bread, 165
Blueberry Coffee Cake, 169
Chocolate Nut Coffee Cake, 170
Corn Bread, 167
Cranberry Bread, 165
Cranberry Buns, 164
Cranberry Scones, 163
Drop Donut Balls, 168
Portuguese Bread, 166

Pumpkin Bread, 167
Pumpkin Seed Bread, 168
Spoon Bread, 166
Strawberry Bread, 170

**Broccoli**
Broccoli au Gratin, 125
Sauteed Vegetables, 108
Stir-Fried Vegetables, 109
Tomato Broccoli Delight, 123
Vegetables in Ranch Dressing, 108

**C**
**Cabbage**
Braised Red Cabbage, 126
Cole Slaw, 138

**Cakes**
Apple Cake, 229
Blueberry Buckle Cake, 211
Blueberry Cakes, 211
Cranberry Cake, 215
Gingerbread, 232
Plum Cake, 231
Pound Cake, 229
Spice Cake, 233

**Carrots**
Carrot Soup, 55
Dilly Carrots, 113

**Champagne**
Champagne Punch, 44

**Cheese**
Apple Cheddar Biscuits, 169
Bacon and Cheese Frittata, 175
Blue Cheese Mashed Potatoes, 120
Brie and Blue Cheese, 31
Cheese Nut Spinach Salad, 139
Cheese Puffs, 30
Cranberry Chutney Brie, 31
Fondue, 32
Hot Brie and Cranberries, 31
Over-Sea Cocktail Special
Pears with Stilton, 32
Raspberry Brie, 30
Tomatoes and Mozzarella, 145

**Cheesecake**
Blackberry Cheesecake, 221
Pumpkin Cheesecake, 227

## Chicken

BBQ Chicken Sandwich, 185
Chicken and Bacon Sandwich, 184
Chicken Breast Salad, 135
Chicken Cheese Sandwich, 188
Chicken Florentine, 85
Chicken Pate, 34
Chicken Pesto Sandwich, 187
Chicken Pie, 86
Chicken Quesadillas, 186
Chicken Salad, 135
Chicken Salad Sandwich, 186
Coq au Vin, 87
Cranberry Chicken Livers, 87
Cranberry Chicken Mold, 88
Curried Chicken Soup, 60
Fettuccine Smoked Chicken, 152
Grilled Chicken Breasts, 85, 88
Grilled Chicken Pita, 185
Mediterranean Chicken, 153
Oriental Chicken Salad, 134
Pate, 33
Pate with Walnuts, 34
Poulet Almondine, 89
Smoked Chicken with Penne, 152
Souffled Chicken Sandwich, 187
Stir-Fry Chicken, 89

## Chocolate

Chocolate Nut Coffee Cake, 170
Chocolate Strawberries, 212
Pumpkin Chocolate Brownies, 235

## Chutney

Faith's Cranberry Chutney, 192

## Cider

Mulled Cider Punch, 47

## Clams

Baked Clams, 20
Clam Chowder, 50
Little Neck Clams, 20
Nantucket Clambake
Quahaug Pie, 177
Seafood Pasta, 148

## Cod

Cod with Mint Salsa, 80
Codfish Balls, 24
Codfish Cakes, 179

## Coffee Cakes

Blueberry Coffee Cake, 169

## Cookies

Blueberry Bar Cookies, 235
Brownies, 240
Date Nut Bars, 238
Gingerbread Men, 239
Mincemeat Cookies, 240
Molasses Cookies, 239
Pumpkin Chocolate Brownies, 235
Rice Flake Cookies, 238

## Corn

Corn and Vegetable Saute, 114
Corn Bread, 167
Corn Chowder, 55
Corn Fritters, 115
Corn Relish, 200
Corn Salad, 146
Corn Salsa, 201

## Couscous

Couscous Cakes, 159
Fall Couscous, 159
Red Pepper Couscous, 158

## Crab

Crab Frittata, 174
Crab Mold, 25
Crab Stuffed Potatoes, 119
Crab Sandwich, 183
Fried Crab Balls, 25
Salmon Shrimp Crab Salad, 130
Seafood Salad, 131
Seafood Sandwich, 184

## Cranberries

Apple Cranberry Pie, 220
Apricot Bread, 165
Braised Spinach, 109
Chocolate Cranberries, 216
Cranberry Apple Conserve, 193
Cranberry Apple Punch, 42
Cranberry Betty, 214
Cranberry Bread, 165
Cranberry Buns, 164
Cranberry Butter, 194
Cranberry Cake, 215
Cranberry Chicken Livers, 87
Cranberry Chicken Mold, 88
Cranberry Chutney, 192

Cranberry Chutney Brie, 31
Cranberry Cocktail, 42
Cranberry Conserve, 193
Cranberry Cooler, 41
Cranberry Cream, 194
Cranberry Custard Pie, 213
Cranberry Delight, 43
Cranberry Duck, 90
Cranberry Mustard, 99
Cranberry Nut Salad, 144
Cranberry Orange Sauce, 192
Cranberry Parfait, 216
Cranberry Pie, 214
Cranberry Pork Chops, 99
Cranberry Punch, 42
Cranberry Roll, 215
Cranberry Salad, 144
Cranberry Sandwiches, 189
Cranberry Sauce, 90, 193
Cranberry Scones, 163
Cranberry Turkey Sandwich, 189
Hot Brie and Cranberries, 31
Hot Spiced Cranberry Punch, 43
Rice with Cranberries, 161
Venison with Cranberry Sauce, 106
Whole Cranberry Sauce, 194

**Cucumbers**
Cucumber and Dill, 116
Cucumber Dill Soup, 59
Cucumber Salad, 146
Minted Cucumbers, 115

**D**
**Desserts**
Apple Cake, 229
Apple Cranberry Pie, 220
Apple Crumb Pie, 219
Apple Crumble, 220
Apple Pudding, 228
Apple Torte, 219
Baked Apples, 228
Blackberry Cheesecake, 221
Blueberry Bar Cookies, 235
Blueberry Buckle Cake, 211
Blueberry Cakes, 211
Blueberry Goodies, 212
Blueberry Grunt, 209
Blueberry Peach Brown Betty, 210
Blueberry Pie, 209
Blueberry Strawberry Tart, 207
Chocolate Cranberries, 216

Chocolate Strawberries, 212
Cracker Pie, 232
Cranberry Betty, 214
Cranberry Cake, 215
Cranberry Custard Pie, 213
Cranberry Parfait, 216
Cranberry Pie, 214
Cranberry Roll, 215
Crepes Suzette, 234
Date Nut Bars, 238
Easy Blueberry Dessert, 208
Elizabeth Gould's Brownies, 240
Fresh Fruit Compote, 230
Fruit with Sour Cream, 216
Ginger Mousse, 231
Gingerbread, 232
Gingerbread Men, 239
Honey Pears, 222
Honeyed Rum Blueberries, 210
Indian Pudding, 227
Indian Tapioca Pudding, 226
Key Lime Pie with Blueberries, 208
Lemon Blackberry Souffle, 224
Lemon Sabayon, 223
Mincemeat Cookies, 240
Molasses Cookies, 239
Pavlova, 226
Peach Blueberry Crisp, 218
Peach Melba, 217
Pound Cake, 229
Plum Cake, 231
Plum Pudding, 230
Pumpkin Cheesecake, 227
Pumpkin Chocolate Brownies, 235
Rhubarb Pie, 221
Rhubarb Strawberry Pie, 222
Rice Flake Cookies, 238
Spice Cake, 233
Spiced Apples, 218
Strawberry Blueberry Trifle, 206
Strawberry Pie, 213
Strawberries Romanoff, 225
Summer Fruit, 217
Tia Maria Parfait, 233

**Dressings**
Herb Salad Dressing, 203
Spinach Dressing, 203

**Drinks**
Champagne Punch, 44
Cranberry Apple Punch, 42

Cranberry Cocktail, 42
Cranberry Cooler, 41
Cranberry Delight, 43
Cranberry Punch, 42
Eggnog, 44
Fish House Punch, 45
Fruit Punch, 46
Hot Spiced Cranberry Punch, 43
Iced Tea, 45
Kir, 46
Lemonade, 44
Little Ga's Fruit Punch, 47
Manhattans, 48
Mrs. Chase's Rum Punch, 43
Mulled Cider Punch, 47
Nantucket Wine Cooler, 41
Old-Fashioned, 48
Party Punch, 47
Planters' Punch, 46
Strawberry Daiquiri, 48

**Duck**
Cranberry Duck, 90
Smoked Duck, 33

**E**
**Egg and Brunch Dishes**
Apple Pancakes, 177
Bacon and Cheese Frittata, 175
Blueberry Pancakes, 178
Blueberry Waffles, 178
Codfish Cakes, 179
Crab Frittata, 174
Creamed Finnan Haddie, 180
Creamed Lobster, 173
Fish Hash, 179
Granola, 176
Lobster Benedict, 172
Quahaug Pie, 177
Sausage and Tomato Quiche, 176
Smoked Salmon Crepes, 180
Spinach and Mushroom Crepes, 173
Spinach Omelet, 174
Summer Omelet, 175

**Eggnog**
Eggnog, 44

**Eggplant**
Baba Ghannooj, 37
Eggplant Casserole, 127
Ratatoille, 126

**Eggs**
Big Ga's Deviled Eggs, 30

**F**
**Finnan Haddie**
Creamed Finnan Haddie, 180

**Flounder**
Fish Chowder, 53
Seafood Casserole, 78
Stuffed Flounder, 76

**Fowl**
Chicken Florentine, 85
Chicken Pie, 86
Coq au Vin, 87
Cranberry Chicken Livers, 87
Cranberry Chicken Mold, 88
Cranberry Duck, 90
Grilled Chicken Breasts, 85, 88
Poulet Almondine, 89
Roast Goose, 91
Roast Turkey, 92
Stir-Fry Chicken, 89

**G**
**Garlic**
Garlic Cream Sauce, 95
Garlic Sauce, 156

**Ginger**
Ginger Mousse, 231
Gingerbread, 232
Gingerbread Men, 239

**Goose**
Roast Goose, 91

**Granola**
Granola, 176

**Grapes**
Grape Conserve, 196, 197

**H**
**Ham**
Deviled Ham Puffs, 28
Ham Mousse, 136
Potato and Ham Soup, 56
Souffled Ham Sandwich, 188

**Herbs and Spices**
Herb Salad Dressing, 203
Rosemary Oil, 204

**Hollandaise**
Easy Hollandaise, 202

**I**
**Ice Cream**
Cranberry Parfait, 216
Peach Melba, 217
Tia Maria Parfait, 233

**J**
**Jams**
Apricot Marmalade, 197
Beach Plum Jelly, 195
Blueberry Jam, 197
Cranberry Apple Conserve, 193
Cranberry Conserve, 193
Grape Conserve, 196, 197
Pumpkin Marmalade, 199
Quince Jam, 195
Red Onion Marmalade, 198
Rose Hip Jam, 196

**L**
**Lamb**
Grilled Lamb, 95
Lamb Patties, 96
Lamb with Port Sauce, 97
Minted Lamb Patties, 97
Lamb with Raspberry Sauce, 96

**Lemons, Limes**
Key Lime Pie with Blueberries, 208
Lemon Blueberry Souffle, 224
Lemon Sabayon with Berries, 223
Lemonade, 44

**Lobster**
Angel Hair Lobster, 149
Bouillabaisse, 52
Broiled Lobster, 74
Creamed Lobster, 173
Curried Lobster Salad, 19, 129
Lobster Benedict, 172
Lobster Bisque, 51
Lobster Dip, 19
Lobster Potato Salad, 130
Lobster Rounds, 19
Lobster Risotto, 157

Lobster Salad, 129
Lobster Sandwich, 183
Lobster Stew, 51
Lobster Thermidor, 75
Lobster with Herbed Mayonnaise, 74
Lobster with Penne, 150
Nantucket Clambake, 69
Pasta with Lobster, 150
Steamed Lobster, 76
Tomato Lobster Bisque, 50

**M**
**Meat and Game**
Beef Nantucket, 103
Beef Oscar, 106
Beef Roulade, 105
Beef Tenderloin, 105
Beef Tournedoes, 104
Cranberry Pork Chops, 99
Curried Pork, 101
Grilled Lamb, 95
Grilled Pork Tenderloin, 98
Grilled Veal Chops, 102
Lamb Patties, 96
Lamb with Port Sauce, 97
Lamb with Raspberry Sauce, 96
Minted Lamb Patties, 97
Pork Picatta, 100
Pork Tenderloin with Cranberry, 99
Roast Pork Tenderloin, 100
Tenderloin with Gorgonzola, 104
Veal with Asparagus, 101
Veal with Mushrooms, 103
Veal with Tomatoes, 102
Venison with Cranberry Sauce, 106

**Menus**
Christmas Dinner, 91
Cranberry Festival, 98
Dinner on the Porch, 131
Easter Dinner, 95
Fishermen's Breakfast, 200
Labor Day Dinner, 63
Ladies Luncheon, 132
Nantucket Clambake, 69
New Year's Eve, 104
Summer Night Dinner, 77
Sunday Brunch, 172
Thanksgiving Dinner, 92

244

**Mincemeat**
Mincemeat Cookies, 240

**Mint**
Mint Sauce, 204

**Mushrooms**
Green Bean Casserole, 110
Mushroom Toasts, 36
Peas and Mushrooms, 117
Spinach and Mushroom Crepes, 173
Veal with Mushrooms, 103

**Mussels**
Mussel Risotto, 158
Mussels and Cod, 68
Mussels and Rice, 67
Mussels Casino, 21
Mussels in Wine Sauce, 67
Mussels Marinara, 68
Nantucket Mussels, 22
Seafood Pasta, 148

**Nuts**
Spiced Nuts, 39

**Onions**
Onion Marmalade, 198
Onion Tagine, 116

**Oranges**
Orange and Spinach Salad, 138
Orange Sauce, 91
Orange Turnips, 117

**Oysters**
Fried Oysters, 83
Oyster Stew, 53

**P**
**Pancakes**
Apple Pancakes, 177
Blueberry Pancakes, 178

**Pastas and Rice**
Angel Hair Pasta with Lobster, 149
Asparagus and Pasta, 154
Couscous Cakes, 159
Dilled Scallops, 151
Fall Cousous, 159
Fettuccine Carbonara, 153
Fettuccine and Smoked Chicken, 152

Green Noodles, 155
Linguine, 157
Lobster Risotto, 157
Lobster with Penne, 150
Mediterranean Chicken, 153
Mussel Rissotto, 158
Pasta Primavera, 155
Pasta with Lobster, 150
Pasta with Spinach Sauce, 154
Pesto Vegetable Pasta, 156
Red Pepper Coucous, 158
Rice with Apricots, 160
Rice with Cranberries, 161
Scallop and Shrimp Toss, 148
Seafood Fettuccine, 149
Seafood Pasta, 148
Smoked Chicken with Penne, 152
Tabbouleh, 161
Vegetable Linguine, 156
Wild Rice, 160

**Peaches**
Blueberry Peach Brown Betty, 210
Pavlova, 226
Peach Blueberry Crisp, 218
Peach Melba, 217
Peach Salsa, 201

**Pears**
Honey Pears, 222
Pears with Stilton, 32

**Peas**
Peas and Mushrooms, 117
Snap Pea Soup, 56

**Peppers**
Red Pepper Couscous, 158
Roasted Peppers, 125

**Pesto**
Lemon Pesto, 133
Pesto Sauce, 23, 202

**Pies**
Apple Cranberry Pie, 220
Apple Crumb Pie, 219
Apple Torte, 219
Blueberry Pie, 209
Blueberry Strawberry Tart, 207
Cracker Pie, 232
Cranberry Custard Pie, 213

Cranberry Pie, 214
Key Lime Pie with Blueberries, 208
Rhubarb Pie, 221
Rhubarb Strawberry Pie, 222
Strawberry Pie, 213

**Pizza**
Vegetarian Pizza, 190

**Plums**
Plum Cake, 231
Plum Pudding, 230

**Pork**
Cranberry Pork Chops, 99
Curried Pork, 101
Grilled Pork Tenderloin, 98
Pork Picatta, 100
Pork Tenderloin, 99
Roast Pork Tenderloin, 100

**Potatoes**
Blue Cheese Mashed Potatoes, 120
Crab Stuffed Potatoes, 119
Garlic Mashed Potatoes, 119
Garlic Potato Cakes, 120
Grilled Vegetables, 114
Lobster and potato Salad, 130
Potato, Garlic, Leek Soup, 57
Potato and Ham Soup, 56
Potato Spinach Croquettes, 118
Potatoes au Gratin, 120
Red Bliss Potatoes, 118
Sweet Potato Casserole, 121

**Pumpkin**
Pumpkin Bread, 167
Pumpkin Cheesecake, 227
Pumpkin Chocolate Brownies, 235
Pumpkin Chutney, 199
Pumpkin Marmalade, 199
Pumpkin Seed Bread, 168
Pumpkin Soup, 57

**Q**
**Quiche**
Sausage and Tomato Quiche, 176

**Quince**
Quince Jam, 195

**R**
**Raspberries**
Lemon Sabayon with Berries, 223
Pavlova, 226
Raspberry Brie, 30
Raspberry Pistacho Sauce, 96
Raspberry Spinach Salad, 139

**Relish**
Corn Relish, 200
Tomato Relish, 200

**Rhubarb**
Rhubarb Chutney, 198
Rhubarb Pie, 221
Rhubarb Strawberry Pie, 222

**Rice**
Peas and Mushrooms, 117
Rice with Cranberries, 161
Wild Rice, 160
Wild Rice with Apricots, 160

**Risotto**
Lobster Risotto, 157
Mussel Risotto, 158

**Rose Hips**
Rose Hip Jam, 196

**Rum**
Honeyed Rum Blueberries, 210
Mrs. Chase's Rum Punch, 43

**S**
**Salads**
Asparagus Salad, 143
Baby Beet Salad, 140
Beet Salad141
Caesar Salad, 136
Cheese and Nut Salad, 139
Chicken Breast Salad, 135
Chicken Salad, 135
Cole Slaw, 138
Corn Salad, 146
Country Salad, 143
Cranberry Salad, 144
Cranberry Nut Salad, 144
Cucumber Salad, 146
Curried Lobster Salad, 129
Grilled Salmon Salad, 133
Ham Mousse, 136

Hot Steak Salad, 134
Lobster and Potato Salad, 130
Lobster Salad, 129
Mixed Greens Salad, 142
Orange Spinach Salad, 138
Oriental Chicken Salad, 134
Raspberry Spinach Salad, 139
Salad Nicoise, 137
Salmon Shrimp Salad, 130
Scallop Salad, 133
Seafood Salad, 131
Shrimp Salad, 132
Spinach Salad, 140
Summer Salad, 141
Tomato and Bread Salad, 145
Tomatoes with Mozzarella, 145
Watercress Salad, 142

**Salmon**
Grilled Salmon Salad, 133
Salmon Blini, 25
Salmon Canapes, 27
Salmon Mousse, 26
Salmon Roll-ups, 26
Salmon Shrimp Crab Salad, 130
Salmon with Horseradish Sauce, 78
Salmon with Spinach, 79, 80
Seafood Baguettes, 27
Seafood Fettuccine, 149
Seafood Salad, 131
Smoked Salmon Crepes, 180

**Salsa**
Black Bean Salsa, 33
Corn Salsa, 201
Mint Salsa, 80
Peach Salsa, 201
Pineapple Salsa, 81
Tomato Avocado Salsa, 63
Tomato Salsa, 79

**Sandwiches**
BBQ Chicken Sandwich, 185
Chicken and Bacon Sandwich, 184
Chicken Cheese Sandwiches, 188
Chicken Pesto Sandwiches, 187
Chicken Quesadillas, 186
Chicken Salad Sandwiches, 186
Crab Sandwich, 183
Cranberry Sandwiches, 189
Cranberry Turkey Sandwiches, 189
Grilled Chicken Pita, 185

Lobster Sandwiches, 183
Scallop Caesar Wrap, 182
Seafood Sandwich, 184
Souffled Chicken Sandwich, 187
Souffled Ham Sandwiches, 188
Swordfish Tacos, 182
Vegetarian Pizza, 190
Vegetarian Sandwich, 190
Veggie Sandwich, 189

**Sauces**
Barbecue Sauce, 203
Beach Plum Sauce, 98
Bearnaise Sauce, 202
Bechamel Sauce, 75
Butter Sauce for Fish, 204
Champagne Basil Sauce, 149
Chive Butter Sauce, 65
Cranberry Sauce, 106
Cream Sauce, 103, 149, 152
Dill Tartar Sauce, 83
Garlic and Butter Sauce, 150
Garlic Cream Sauce, 95
Garlic Wine Sauce, 156
Gorgonzola Port Sauce, 104
Herb Cream Sauce, 155
Herbed Mayonnaise, 74
Hollandaise Sauce, 172, 202
Horseradish Sauce, 78
Lobster Cream Sauce, 71
Mint Sauce, 97, 204
Ouzo Cream Sauce, 153
Parmesan Cream Sauce, 157
Pesto, 23, 27, 202
Port Sauce, 97
Raspberry Pistachio Sauce, 96
Tomato Salsa, 79, 201
Spinach Sauce, 66, 154
Tartar Sauce, 201

**Sausage**
Sausage and Tomato Quiche, 176

**Scallops**
Bacon Wrapped Scallops, 23
Bay Scallops in Pastry, 71
Coquilles, 72
Dilled Scallops, 151
Jambalaya, 82
Scallop and Shrimp Toss, 148
Scallop Caesar Wrap, 182
Scallop Casserole, 73

Scallop Ceviche, 72
Seafood Pasta, 148
Scallop Salad, 133
Scallop Shrimp Toss, 148
Scallop Stew, 54
Scallops Almondine, 70
Scallops in Wine Sauce, 73
Scallops with Dill Sauce, 22
Seafood Fettuccine, 149
Seafood Salad, 131
Skewered Scallops, 70
Smoked Scallops with Pesto, 23

## Seafood
Baked Bluefish, 77
Bay Scallops in Puff Pastry, 71
Broiled Lobster, 74
Cod with Mint Salsa, 80
Coquilles, 72
Crab Sandwich, 183
Curried Lobster Salad, 129
Fried Oysters, 83
Garlicy Shrimp, 83
Grilled Salmon Salad, 133
Grilled Swordfish, 63
Grilled Swordfish with Salsa, 63
Jambalaya, 82
Lobster and Potato Salad, 130
Lobster with Herbed Mayonnaise, 74
Lobster Salad, 129
Lobster Sandwich, 183
Lobster Thermidor, 75
Mussels and Cod, 68
Mussels and Rice, 67
Mussels in Wine Sauce, 67
Mussels Marinara, 68
Nantucket Clambake, 69
Salmon and Spinach, 80
Salmon Shrimp Crab Salad, 130
Salmon with Horseradish, 78
Salmon with Spinach, 79
Scallop Casserole, 73
Scallop Caesar Wrap, 182
Scallop Ceviche, 72
Scallop Salad, 133
Scallop Shrimp Toss, 148
Scallops Almondine, 70
Scallops in Wine Sauce, 73
Seafood Casserole, 78
Seafood Fettuccine, 149
Seafood Pasta, 148
Seafood Salad, 131

Seafood Sandwich, 184
Skewered Scallops, 70
Skewered Swordfish, 64
Steamed Lobster, 76
Stuffed Flounder, 76
Swordfish Tacos, 182
Swordfish with Basil Butter, 64
Swordfish with Chive Butter, 64
Swordfish with Island Sauce, 65
Swordfish with Spinach Sauce, 66
Tuna with Mango, 81
Tuna with Pineapple Salsa, 81
Tuna with Mushrooms, 82

## Shrimp
Garlicy Shrimp, 83
Jambalaya, 82
Salmon Shrimp Crab Salad, 130
Scallop and Shrimp Toss, 148
Seafood Fettuccine, 149
Shrimp Salad, 132

## Souffles
Lemon Blueberry Souffle, 224

## Soups
Bouillabaisse, 52
Carrot Soup, 55
Clam Chowder, 50
Corn Chowder, 55
Cream of Asparagus Soup, 60
Cucumber Dill Soup, 59
Curried Squash Soup, 58
Curried Chicken Soup, 60
Fish Chowder, 53
Fruit Soup, 59
Gazpacho, 54
Harvest Squash Soup, 58
Lobster Bisque, 51
Lobster Stew, 51
Oyster Stew, 53
Potato and Ham Soup, 56
Potato Garlic, Leek Soup, 57
Pumpkin Soup, 57
Scallop Stew, 54
Snap Pea Soup, 56
Tomato Lobster Bisque, 50

## Spinach
Baby Spinach Fingers, 34
Braised Spinach, 109
Cheese Nut Spinach Salad, 139

Orange and Spinach Salad, 138
Pasta with Spinach Sauce, 154
Potato Spinach Croquettes, 118
Raspberry Spinach Salad, 139
Sauteed Spinach, 109
Spinach and Mushroom Crepes, 173
Spinach Cheesecake, 35
Spinach Dip, 35
Spinach Dressing, 203
Spinach Omelet. 174
Spinach Torta, 110
Stir-fried Vegetables, 109

**Squash**
Courge Squash, 121
Curried Squash Soup, 58
Grilled Vegetables, 114
Harvest Squash Soup, 58
Sauteed Vegetables, 108

**Strawberries**
Blueberry Strawberry Tart, 207
Chocolate Strawberries, 212
Fruit Soup, 59
Fruit with Sour Cream, 216
Rhubarb Strawberry Pie, 222
Strawberries Romanoff, 225
Strawberry Blueberry Trifle, 206
Strawberry Bread, 170
Strawberry Daiquiri, 48
Strawberry Pie, 213

**Stuffing**
Herb Bread Stuffing, 93
Sausage Stuffing, 92

**Sweet Potatoes**
Sweet Potato Casserole, 121

**Swordfish**
Grilled Swordfish, 63
Grilled Swordfish with Salsa, 63
Skewered Swordfish, 64
Swordfish Blinis, 24
Swordfish Tacos, 182
Swordfish with Basil Butter, 64
Swordfish with Chive Butter, 65
Swordfish with Island Sauce, 65
Swordfish with Spinach Sauce, 66

**T**
**Tapioca**
Indian Tapioca Pudding, 226

**Tartar Sauce**
Fried Oysters with Tartar Sauce, 83
Tartar Sauce, 201

**Tea**
Iced Tea, 45

**Tomatoes**
Gazpacho, 54
Sausage and Tomato Quiche, 176
Sauteed Vegetables, 108
Scalloped Tomatoes, 123
Stewed Tomatoes, 122
Tomato and Bread Salad, 145
Tomato Broccoli Delight, 123
Tomato Lobster Bisque, 50
Tomato Pudding, 124
Tomato Relish, 200
Tomato Tart, 124
Tomatoes and Mozzarella, 145
Veal with Tomatoes, 102

**Trifle**
Strawberry Blueberry Trifle, 206

**Tuna**
Salad Nicoise, 137
Tuna with Mango Butter, 81
Tuna with Salsa, 81
Tuna with Mushrooms, 82

**Turkey**
Cranberry Turkey Sandwich, 189
Roast Turkey, 92

**Turnips**
Orange Turnips, 117

**V**
**Veal**
Grilled Veal Chops, 102
Veal with Asparagus, 101
Veal with Mushrooms, 103
Veal with Tomatoes, 102

**Vegetables**
Asparagus Salad, 143
Asparagus Tart, 122
Blue Cheese Mashed Potatoes, 120
Braised Red Cabbage, 126
Braised Spinach, 109
Broccoli au Gratin, 125
Corn and Vegetable Saute, 114
Corn Fritters, 115
Courge Squash, 121
Crab Stuffed Potatoes, 119
Crudites, 38
Cucumber and Dill, 116
Dilly Carrots, 113
Dilly Green Beans, 112
Eggplant Casserole, 127
Garlic Mashed Potatoes, 119
Garlic Potato Cakes, 120
Green Bean Casserole, 111
Green Beans and Apples, 111
Green Beans and Mushrooms, 110
Green Beans with Bacon, 112
Grilled Vegetables, 114
Minted Cucumbers, 115
Onion Tagine, 116
Orange Turnips, 117
Peas and Mushrooms, 117
Potato Spinach Croquettes, 118
Potatoes au Gratin, 120
Ratatoille, 126
Red Bliss Potatoes, 118
Roasted Peppers, 125
Sauteed Spinach, 109
Sauteed Vegetables, 108
Scalloped Tomatoes, 123
Spinach Torta, 110
Vegetables in Ranch Dressing, 108

Stewed Tomatoes, 122
Stir-Fried Vegetables, 109
Stuffed Vegetables, 113
Sweet Potato Casserole, 121
Tomato Broccoli Delight, 123
Tomato and Bread Salad, 145
Tomato Pudding, 124
Tomato Tart, 124
Tomatoes and Mozzarella, 145
Vegetable Cheesecake, 36
Vegetables in Ranch Dressing, 108
Vegetarian Pizza, 190
Vegetarian Sandwich, 190
Veggie Sandwich, 189

**Venison**
Venison with Cranberry Sauce, 106

**W**
**Watercress**
Watercress Salad, 142

**Watermelon**
Summer Fruit, 217

**Z**
**Zucchini**
Grilled Vegetables, 114
Pesto Vegetable Pasta, 156
Sauteed Vegetables, 108
Stir-Fried Vegetables, 109
Stuffed Vegetables, 113
Vegetable Linguine, 156
Vegetables in Ranch Dressing, 108

## About the Author and Photographer

Katie Barney Moose, born in Baltimore, is a descendant of the Clagett (Claggett) family of Maryland, and many old New England whaling families.

She has lived in many of the U.S.' great culinary, architectural, historical and waterside gems besides Annapolis - New Castle, DE; Newport and Providence, RI; Cold Spring Harbor, NY; San Francisco; Philadelphia; Greenwich, CT; Alexandria, VA; Washington, DC; and New York City. She and her family maintain homes on Nantucket Island.

Mrs. Moose is in the process of publishing a series of regional cookbooks, and guidebooks on the different regions of the Chesapeake Bay. She was the co-author of "The Best of Newport, the Newport Guidebook", several publications on the fiber optic telecommunications business, and is a consultant on international business and protocol. Her hobbies, beside gourmet cooking and fine wines, include history, sailing, genealogy, theology and travel.

# *Order Form for Conduit Press Books*

Please send me____ copies of Nantucket's Bounty @ $17.95

Please send me ____ copies of Chesapeake's Bounty @ $16.95

Please send me____ copies of Annapolis: The Guidebook @ $13.95

Please send me____ copies of Eastern Shore of Maryland: The Guidebook @ $15.95

Add postage first book @ $3.00____
Postage for each additional book to same address @ $1.00____
Gift wrap per book @$2.00____
Total Order_____

❑   Check or money order enclosed
❑   Make check payable to Conduit Press
❑   Please personalize to:

Mail to:

Conduit Press
111 Conduit Street
Annapolis, MD 21401

Ship the Cookbook to:

Name_____

Address_____

_____

Telephone_____

For further information please
•   Call 410-280-5272
•   Fax 410-263-5380
•   E-mail kamoose@erols.com